DON'T PANIC . . .
About Disappointing A-level Results and Highers

by
Fiona Smith

Trotman and Company Limited

The author wishes to thank Jenny Harrison and Claire Boyling for typing the manuscript of this book.

DON'T PANIC

... about disappointing A-level results/Highers

Fiona Smith

This edition published in 1989 in Great Britain by
Trotman and Company Limited
12–14 Hill Rise, Richmond, Surrey TW10 6UA

© Trotman and Company Ltd

ISBN 0 85660 1403

Cover illustration by Jane Eccles

Typeset by Wessex Typesetters
(Division of The Eastern Press Ltd)
Frome, Somerset

Reproduced, Printed and Bound in Great Britain by
The Eastern Press Ltd., Reading

Contents

An introduction for students

You will probably never experience a more uncertain summer than this – waiting for the results of your final school examinations. Poised on the brink of your adult life, the suspense of these weeks can seem intolerable. Perhaps you have picked up this book during that interminable period with the intention of arming yourself with alternatives should your chosen path no longer be open to you, or you may in fact have already received disappointing results which have prompted you to rethink your future. Whichever of these is your situation this book is intended for you. It aims, at a time when your morale may be low, to boost your confidence, to encourage you not to panic, and to help you adopt a clear-sighted approach to your particular situation.

You will be guided through a Ten Point Plan of Action whose purpose will be two-fold: to offer sound practical advice about the options that are available to you and to help you face and come to terms with personal reactions to your disappointment.

In summary the Plan covers:

1. **How to survive examination disappointment.** Your initial reactions and those of parents, family and friends. These can be painful and embarrassing and coming to terms with a sense of 'failure' and feelings of inadequacy are essential ingredients towards a positive rethink about your future.

2. **Assess the situation.** It would be a mistake to embark on a fresh course of action without a review of what went wrong in the first instance. An assessment of the reasons for disappointing results is vital – if you know the reasons you stand a much better chance of not being disappointed in your chosen course of action.

3. **Where can I look for help?** Once you are ready to face the world you will want to lose no time in making contact with the person or institution best able to help you in your present needs. Whom to approach, and how, will be a priority.

4. **What are the options?** To retake or not to retake. To try for an alternative course. To get a job. To take time off. These are some of the possibilities which have doubtless crossed your mind and you will want to explore.

5. **Are retakes worth it?** For some this will be the right move, but it is by no means the solution for all. You will need informed

advice as to whether this is the right course of action for you.

6. **Alternative courses.** What else can you do with your present results? You may be unaware of the wide range of alternative courses available to you. These could widen your horizons, and open up new possibilities.

7. **What about a job?** The world of work may beckon, but what are the prospects, and will your qualifications fit you for a training scheme?

8. **Handling interviews – Positive thinking.** After a setback in examinations there can be special difficulties attached to interviews for jobs or college places. Convince yourself that you are *not* a 'failure' and you will be on the way to convincing others.

9. **Further counselling.** If, having considered all these options you are still in a state of indecision, you should consider further careers counselling.

10. **Taking time off.** Although a complete break from study may appear to be the obvious choice, and can be a fruitful experience, it should be a positive decision.

Your anxieties are likely to be reflected by your parents who will doubtless share your concern. They may not, however, be aware of the range of opportunities open to you and may see your results in terms of 'failure'. The points covered in this book should provide the information you require to present the situation to your parents and discuss its implications.

So make a start now on your campaign of action to turn what you may see at the moment as 'failure' into success, and by the time you have finished reading Point 1: How to Survive Examination Disappointment, you will, I hope, realise that you are certainly not a 'failure'.

An introduction for parents

For many parents the worry and the pressures of final school examinations – that is A-levels, or in Scotland – H Grades – can prove to be almost as great as they are for their student sons and daughters. It may well be such an experience which has prompted you to turn to this book for guidance in anticipation of, or when actually faced by, the reality of disappointing results.

You will doubtless be anxious to give as much support as possible to your son or daughter at a difficult time but may be bewildered and unsure of how best to advise them. Changes in education since your own schooldays perhaps make you feel out of touch with your child's academic life. In some schools too there may be little parent-teacher contact, and certainly as students progress through school parental involvement usually becomes much more limited.

The highly competitive nature of entry to higher education and the narrow margin between acceptance onto a course or rejection leave little leeway when it comes to examination results. Employers too require qualifications which even a decade ago would have been less stringent. Your aspirations for your offspring could therefore be unrealistic in the light of current requirements. A young person's early scholastic promise may diminish as competition becomes stiffer in secondary school and subjects require more in-depth study. Expectations by schools and parents may be beyond the capabilities of some pupils who find it an uphill struggle to grapple with their subjects.

There are, however, promising alternatives, and to be armed with alternative courses of action if results do prove disappointing is the most positive approach for any parent. Should you be reading this prior to results, now is the time to sow the seeds of encouragement and to discuss possible changes.

When faced by disappointing results your son or daughter may feel that you have been let down and that they are a 'failure' in your eyes – by the time you have read Chapter 1 in this book you should be convinced, and be able to convince your son or daughter, just how very inappropriate that hurtful label 'failure' is. In the meantime, both emotional and practical support are required to weather the storm. Once the initial reactions have been allowed to subside, reassurance and encouragement to explore the options available should be a priority.

There are options, and it is the aim of this book to explore these options and to strike a note of optimism. Your positive and supportive attitude will be a vital factor in helping your son or daughter to cope with disappointment and to take the positive steps required to build a successful future.

How to survive examination disappointment

Your examination results have let you down and your future seems
uncertain. That cherished offer of a place in higher education, or
the promising job prospect, appears to have eluded you. Your
dreams are shattered. Perhaps you received the news in a state of
disbelief, or it may be but the realisation of your worst fears.
Whether you secretly anticipated this outcome, or whether it has
come as a complete shock, you are likely to be overwhelmed by
feelings of anxiety about your situation. You probably feel at a
loss – bewildered and confused. You are aware of the need to
rethink your future and yet you are assailed by a turmoil of
conflicting emotions.

Try not to panic. This is a stressful experience for you. But
once you have come to terms with the situation and to your
reactions to that situation, you will be in a position to take positive
steps to rebuild your future.

It is all very well, you may say, to talk in terms of a positive
approach, but you are undoubtedly feeling at a low ebb. After all,
for several years you have been encouraged to believe that A-level
achievement is of paramount importance. Urged by parents and
teachers alike you have devoted so much time and energy to your
studies when alternative attractions have beckoned, that you cannot
be blamed for wondering whether it has all been a pointless exercise.
Careers literature and college prospectuses, with their bland
assumptions of achievement, leave students ill-prepared for 'failure'.
Before embarking on any important decisions you need to come to
terms with the situation and try to understand your natural reactions.
And the first thing to do is to tackle that word 'failure'.

Positive thinking

No matter what you may think at the moment, or what your friends
or parents may think, you are *not* a 'failure'. You have taken and
stuck with, what was almost certainly, a two year course studying
for A-levels – and that in itself is an achievement which says
something positive about you. And, in the process, you have learned
a great deal and benefited as a person.

5

But, you may say, "I didn't get a place at university, poly or college". That does *not*, I repeat, make you a 'failure'. Rather you are in the *majority* of young people of your age. Of those who apply for places on university courses less than 44 per cent succeed. And if nearly 200,000 young people of your age begin various courses of higher education each year, at a whole range of institutions – not just universities, polytechnics and colleges and institutes of higher education, there are over 500,000 belonging to the same age group who do not. You see – you are in an even *bigger* majority. Besides which, we haven't yet begun to explore all the possibilities which remain for you to *still* enter higher education.

To be talking about 'failure' is illogical. Do you *seriously* consider two-thirds of your age group to be 'failures'?

You have a lot to offer. There is all you have learned while you were studying for A-levels or Highers. And – of greater value than plain facts – you will have learned the skills of interpretation and of presentation and the basics of 'how to learn'. Whether you realise it or not, you have already got more to offer than the majority of young people of your age.

Why?

There is a temptation to indulge in post-mortems – to reflect on what the outcome might have been if only it had not been your misfortune to be faced with exam questions on topics which you had not covered adequately in your revision. While it is, of course, very frustrating to feel that you were unlucky, it is too late to turn the clock back and a pointless waste of time to linger long on that aspect.

It is natural to blame others – parents and teachers being the most likely candidates. You may think that inadequate teaching or a personality clash with a teacher was the source of the problem, and there can sometimes be justification for these beliefs. If results have in general been poor in a certain subject in your school, it could point to unsatisfactory teaching. But before jumping to conclusions, it is as well to see the results in the context of the *entire* school, and not just your form which may not have been the highest ability group. The head of your school will doubtless take appropriate action in the face of a complete disaster in a particular subject, though unfortunately it may be too late for you.

If you have heartily disliked, or been disliked by, a teacher it could have contributed to lack of interest and motivation in a subject. The most positive step you can take now is to ensure that you do not allow future relationships with teaching staff at your next place of study to have a detrimental effect on your performance. There are bound to be people in authority at school, in college or at work whom you do not particularly like but with whom you need to strike up a working relationship.

Family and friends

It is your parents and family who will probably be the first to share your news and the first to offer sympathy or criticism. If, as is usual, they are supportive, they will be invaluable allies ready to share your problem and help you work towards its solution. Relationships with parents can however be strained as both you and they come to terms with the disappointment. Words of consolation or encouragement may only meet with your resentment. After all, it's not their 'failure', and you probably feel that nobody really understands the depth of your despair.

Recriminations, both expressed and implied, can rub salt in the wound. Perhaps you did spend rather too much time on the sports field or at the disco, but you couldn't after all be expected to devote all the days of your youth to study! Although they may not express it, parents often blame themselves and question whether their choice of school was wrong, or their ambitions for you unrealistic. Parents can be seen to be at fault for many reasons, and their expectations become a source of conflict. It would be a great pity to sour a hitherto good relationship with your parents by blaming them for your present predicament. On the other hand if relations have been strained lately, your disappointment could have the effect of drawing you closer together again. And try not to discount suggestions by your parents and their friends who may well have experienced such a situation before.

Parents are not the only family members with whom you have to relate. Grandparents, aunts and uncles, brothers and sisters who will have had their expectations of you have to be faced. To have seen an older brother or sister sail through life ahead of you with great success can be a bitter pill to swallow when faced with your present lack of success. Perhaps just as painful is when family expectations of your potential have been high and have not now been realised. Comparisons are not confined to brothers and sisters – cousins too can be held up as yardsticks of achievement. Comparisons with others can give a false impression of your own worth. So, you may have to gently remind relatives that you are not Cousin Jack but a person with your own skills and virtues and the promise of your own distinct contribution to life.

To hide like an ostrich and retreat to the confines of your room may be your way of dealing with the problem and while it offers temporary solace, it is no permanent solution. It is tempting to shun friends and acquaintances whose questions, spoken or unspoken, about your examination results may cause acute embarrassment. The success of classmates with their air of optimism is difficult to bear without feeling envious at their good fortune and apparent easy success. Their plans for what appears to be a rosy future stand out in stark contrast to the uncertainty of yours. It is therefore only natural to feel left out and a bit resentful. You may be inclined to seek consolation in the company of others in a similar situation to your own – remember you are in the majority – and while their companionship may fit the needs of the moment, you will be surprised how quickly you will almost certainly feel at ease again in your old friendships. But if not the changes that are in store for you as you leave school will in any case include embarking on new friendships and perhaps losing contact with some school friends.

Your feelings

It is not unusual to be assailed by feelings of inadequacy. It is after all a testing time for you. This may be the first real disappointment in your life and your anger and frustration should not be underestimated. How you cope now can, however, help you learn to face future difficulties. If, rather than succumbing to feelings of self-pity and envy, you determine to overcome this setback you could even turn it to your advantage.

Don't be deluded into thinking that the problem will sort itself out. It will not. A determined effort on your part to see a reversal in your fortunes will be necessary. It will not be easy, but you will be rewarded by immense satisfaction if you can make a success of this next stage in your life, in spite of what has happened.

So, start by making a supreme effort to rid yourself of negative emotions. It would be as well if you could try to put your position into perspective. As you've just read, your situation is certainly not unique. Many students fall short of the requirements for their chosen course and go on to carve out a successful future for themselves. It is important to try to rebuild your self-confidence in preparation for a positive approach. It may seem a small consolation at the minute but do try to remember that you are among the small percentage of the population who have reached such a high standard of education. You have a record of academic achievement, even if your present attainment falls short of expectation. Don't, whatever you do, lose sight of all that you have *already* achieved.

When so much importance appears to be placed on paper qualifications, it may be difficult to see beyond academic ability. But take heart! Many well-known figures have no imposing string of A-levels or Highers to their name. Your own parents, and relations too, may well have had their examination difficulties in the past. Doubtless you have attributes other than the merely academic. Accept the encouragement of family and friends graciously and think positively.

Reassessment

Now is the time for a personal reappraisal and a reassessment of your aims and ambitions – an opportunity to question assumptions about your objectives for the future. However disinclined you may be to accept a change in direction from your chosen course it is perhaps necessary, and may even, after the initial shock, prove exciting!

Assess the situation

Now that the initial shock of your results is behind you and you
are beginning to come to terms with what has happened, the time
is ripe to assess the situation. It may not be as bad as you first
imagined. Is your disappointment absolute? Have you in fact failed
each subject that you attempted, or have you achieved passes, but
with grades lower than required for your chosen course? Should
you have narrowly missed the grades expected of you for a university
or polytechnic place, for example, they might still be disposed to
confirm your offer, depending on the availabiliy of places. It is
certainly worth making contact with the institutions concerned. An
alternative offer is a possibility even if your results fall short of the
requirement for your original choice. Don't assume that all is lost
until you have checked with the admissions staff. Provided that
you have achieved the general entry requirements and have almost
reached the target you might still be considered. Admissions tutors
are of course under considerable pressure at this time as they piece
together the jigsaw of their student intake, and it would therefore
be unrealistic to expect an immediate response, but do make contact.
Your school may be helpful in this matter with a member of staff
in a position to speak up in your favour.

It could be that illness or severe family problems at examination
time were contributory factors in your disappointing results. A
member of staff could point this out for you and you may receive
sympathetic consideration if backed by a medical certificate. To be
realistic, though; it is unlikely that such reasons will tip the scales
in your favour if you did not take appropriate action at the time of
your examinations.

Once certain that your *chosen* course is indeed unattainable,
take stock of the situation. A calm and clear-sighted approach is
essential. If you have anticipated this eventuality you may already
have an embryonic plan in mind. NOW is the time to activate it.
If, however, you had 'hoped for the best', you are likely to have to
do some rethinking – you'll need to consider alternative courses,
get involved with 'Clearing', if that is appropriate, and so on. And
you will find details of these options in *Point 3: Where Can I Look
For Help?* But . . . before moving forward you would do well to
cast a backward glance into the past – that is, your own past.

There are reasons for your present predicament, reasons of which you may be only too well aware. These could, however, be but the tip of the iceberg. Like a detective you must search for clues that lie submerged beneath the surface.

A superficial assessment could fail to provide you with the solution to the problem. It is in your own interests, therefore, to give some time and thought to the real reasons for your disappointment. It need not be too time-consuming as prompt action may be required for any alternative decision, for example, obtaining a course through Clearing. But it must be constructive, for to ignore the *root* of the problem could lead to the wrong choice now and further similar setbacks in the future. The following questions might provide a framework for constructive thought.

1. Why did it happen?
2. What does it tell me about myself and my plans?
3. Is it likely to happen again because I have chosen an inappropriate path?

Clues to these questions lie not only in your education but in you yourself. It would be valuable, therefore, to set out on a quest for self-knowledge. Enlist the help of family and friends if you would find it useful. Scrutinise your educational background first of all and examine the reasons for your choice of subjects, and particularly those in which you under-achieved.

Choice of A-levels and AS-levels/Highers

1. Liked subject and good at it

You liked a subject and thought that you were good at it, and yet you did not achieve. It could be that you were over-confident, and concentrated too hard on other subjects to the detriment of your 'best' subject. You could of course not have been as good as you were encouraged to believe – were you, for example, a 'high flier' in the subject among many or just a few at your school. And if you were 'good' compared with only a very small group, what was *their* standard? Look at the results of the others at school as this could be indicative of insufficient preparation in your subject.

The educational assessment

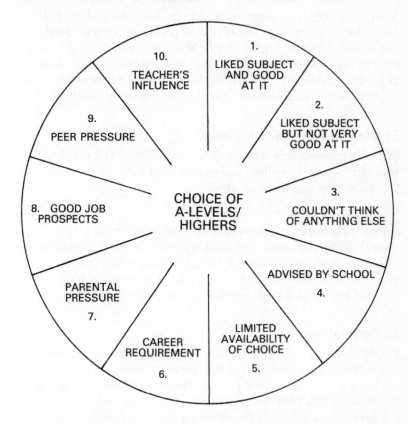

2. Liked subject but not very good at it

While a liking for a subject can undoubtedly contribute to success in it, it does not always lead to success.

3. Couldn't think of anything else

Sometimes, having made the initial choice of subjects it is difficult to select the remainder. No logical solution offers itself and you are left with an unappealing selection. Did the subject that let you down fall into this category?

4. Advised by the school

Your school head, tutor, or careers adviser may have encouraged you to follow a certain course of study against your own inclination if it appeared to offer a better chance of success. You could therefore have had no real interest in the subject and little motivation. Your O-levels, GCSEs or O grades could also have given a false impression of your ability to succeed in a subject when studied in depth. Was this the case?

5. Limited availability of choice

Schools can impose restrictions on what combination of subjects they offer according to their size and the availability of teaching. Did yours give you a limited choice?

6. Career requirement

An ambition to pursue a certain career may have directed your choice of subject. Some subjects are necessary for entry to particular courses of study; you could not, for example, normally take an engineering degree without A-level maths. A poor result in an essential subject could indicate that you need to rethink your original career choice.

7. Parental pressure

Parents can have ambitions for their offspring which are unrealistic in the light of their abilities and the current academic requirements. There may have been strong pressures to follow in the footsteps of, for instance, a medical family, or to join the family firm. Encouragement to study subjects with a view to a specific career could, in your case, have been misplaced.

8. Good job prospects

Job popularity goes in phases, with prestige professions and the lure of high financial reward encouraging the lemming-like pursuit of favoured occupations. Influenced to believe that success lies in the attainment of, for example, an accountancy or law degree, you may have been one of the many chasing over-subscribed courses with entry requirements beyond your capabilities.

9. Peer pressure

To study the same subject as your friends may have had a strong appeal and persuaded you to follow a path which did not really suit your individual needs.

10. Teachers' influence

While a liking for a teacher can undoubtedly spark off a great interest in a subject, it will not be sufficient if your innate ability does not lie in that direction. Conversely, a dislike of a teacher might cause you to drop a subject in which you could have been successful.

Conclusions

Hopefully a few answers will have emerged to cast some light on the reasons for your results. Probe further into your educational background, for more discoveries may yet be in store.

Were you possibly affected by frequent changes of school which set you back each time you moved? Even one move at a crucial time could mean that you missed vital teaching and never quite got to grips with the basics in a subject. Constant changes of teacher, or a new teacher at a particularly important time could also have caused setbacks; some students take longer than others to adapt to new teaching methods or a different approach to a subject. On the other hand boredom can set in if you have been in the same establishment for many years. Dull routine breeds apathy and lack of enthusiasm. This may have been your lot – not conducive to good results!

The school itself could have been inappropriate for your needs. In some schools great emphasis is laid on success in certain areas of school life, such as sport or artistic pursuits, and the pressure to succeed in the popular aspects of the school could be detrimental to the study of others.

The personal assessment

Whatever conclusion you reach about the educational aspect it will provide only one part of the story. To shed more light on the subject examine yourself. You may have to face a few unpalatable truths, but without a self-assessment you will risk a repetition of the problem. Once again ask yourself some searching questions.

The personal assessment

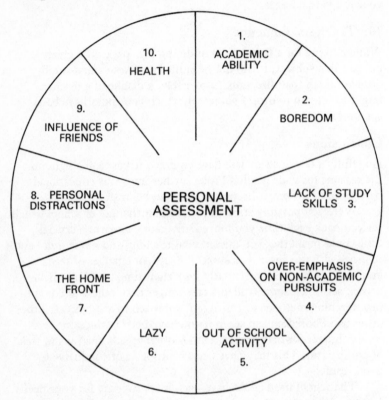

1. Academic ability

Was it a struggle for you to understand your subjects and to keep up with other students? Did you find that your academic achievement deteriorated as you progressed through school, in spite of working to the best of your ability? It could be that either your choice of subjects was not compatible with your abilities or that your talents lie in other directions.

2. Boredom

A bored student rarely reaches his or her true potential. If your A-levels bored you, either your choice of course was wrong or the teaching did not inspire.

3. Lack of study skills

It is not unusual to think that you are working well and yet to fail
to cover the work adequately through lack of organisation. Time
spent sitting at your books can be time wasted if it is not used
constructively. Shorter periods with a break can be more rewarding
than long unbroken stretches where the mind wanders into a time-
wasting daydream.

4. Over-emphasis on 'non-academic' school pursuits

A place in the hockey or rugby team or a part in a play can assume
overwhelming proportions and can be very time-consuming.
Pressure to take part in frequent training sessions or rehearsals
leaves a student short of time for study. Your abilities may of
course lie in these areas and prove to be a true reflection of where
you should in fact be directing your future.

5. Out-of-school activity

While concentration on academic study to the exclusion of all other
interests is undoubtedly narrow and not really to be recommended,
when it comes to final school examinations *too many* interests and
commitments can be distracting. There are some people who seem
to be able to cope well with everything, but for most ordinary
mortals it is necessary to curtail some activities for the pre-
examination period. A Saturday job, regular evening or weekend
interests, clubs and discos all eat into valuable study time. Was
this your problem?

6. Lazy

If in your heart of hearts you can admit that this was your weakness,
the remedy lies in your own hands.

7. The home front

Family problems do impinge on your work and can have a
devastating effect. Relationships within the family are not always
conducive to a calm atmosphere, and family arguments may have
taken their toll. You may not have been fortunate enough to have
a quiet place in which to study and constant distractions of noise or
television can be very off-putting.

8. Personal distractions

Close emotional involvement with one particular person can be distracting. It is difficult to concentrate on your work if your thoughts are constantly dominated by such a personal relationship.

9. The influence of friends

Some friends can have an unfortunate influence – their values are at odds with those of your family and you are torn between your wish to conform to their standards and the restraints imposed by your upbringing. This is a treacherous breeding-ground for conflict. Friends and acquaintances too who have left school and given up their studies appear to have a freedom that you lack, and cast doubt on the point of your studies. Did this happen to you?

10. Health

Not everyone is blessed with boundless energy and good health. If your health is below par or you have a chronic problem you will under-achieve. Those who need little sleep fit more into their lives, while the day is shorter for those who require a good night's rest. Illness before or during examinations can but have a detrimental effect on examination performance. Was poor health at the root of your problems?

Conclusion

While this is not an exhaustive list of questions – friends, family and you yourself can doubtless enlarge upon it – it should provide the necessary clues from which to draw conclusions about why it happened.

The solution to your dilemma must now be sought. If it appears that you have made a choice of subjects at variance with your true interests or abilities you will clearly wish to avoid a repetition of that mistake. Should you have been strongly influenced by teachers or parents, now may be the time for a frank discussion with them about where you have gone wrong and why. It will be your responsibility to ensure that you are not guided yet again into an inappropriate path. After all, it is you who must live with the consequences of these decisions.

And if you conclude that you lacked motivation or allowed

non-academic pursuits or personal relationships to dominate your life you must decide where your priorities lie.

Your future success will depend on how you tackle this assessment you have made of your situation. While it will not provide an immediate solution, if you can pinpoint the *reasons* for your disappointing results the first steps towards a fresh approach to your future will have been taken.

Point 3

Where can I look for help?

With your voyage of self-discovery behind you, prepare to embark
on the next stage of your journey along the road to a successful
future. The general direction in which you should be heading will
be determined by the conclusions you have reached in your
assessment of the underlying reasons for your results. A *modified*
change of course may be all that is required, or it may now be clear
that it is imperative to go back to the drawing board and start again
from scratch. Set out, therefore, on a fact-finding mission so that,
armed with the necessary information you can plot your course,
and enlist the help of those who can pilot you through the turbulent
waters ahead.

It is vital to be at hand so that you are on the spot to make
personal contact with those whose assistance you require or to give
an immediate response to an offer from a Clearing House or a
college. You may feel that a good holiday is what you really need
to cheer you up but don't be tempted to retreat to a Hebridean
island where you will be incommunicado! Staying at home is the
best option.

The first logical port of call should be your school or college
which, although closed for holidays, may operate a rescue service
for students in need at this time. Guidance from a teacher or careers
adviser who knows you well and is experienced in dealing with those
in a predicament such as yours could be invaluable. A telephone
call will quickly establish whether such help is at hand. Your best
point of contact would be a member of staff who has previously
been involved in your decision-making process and who knows you
from both an academic and a personal point of view. Occasionally,
if the result of any subject is so completely unexpected by both
student and school, an appeal might be considered, but this is a
lengthy procedure and is not often recommended.

Many schools do not, however, have staff available for
consultation during the holidays and, even if yours does, you
should certainly also be aware of other sources of assistance. It will
eventually be up to you to take the necessary action to secure your
chosen course or job and you cannot really do this if you lack
information.

Your school may be firmly shut, but your local careers office will have an open door. A 'crisis crew' is always at hand when results come out to cope with students in just such a situation as yours. It offers a lifeline – AFEIS (Advanced Further Education Information Service) – to students in distress, and what's more the service is free. In August and September of each year, the local authority officers of AFEIS are geared up to deal with the difficulties faced by students in the aftermath of examination results, and there should be an AFEIS contact whom you can consult within reasonable reach of your home. All you have to do is to ring up or go into the office and make an appointment for a chat. You will find the address and telephone number of your local careers office under 'Careers Service' in the telephone directory. Should you already have established contact with an adviser through a previous interview at school you might like to speak to that person in the first instance. The careers advisers will have dealt with your type of problem on innumerable occasions and will be in a position not only to give practical advice, but to discuss the implications of pursuing certain courses of action. They will have full information about higher education courses including up-to-date details of entry requirements, vacancies and procedures, and can also advise on how to set about finding employment. It makes sense to make use of the wealth of information and expertise available. Students in Scotland will find this service at their local careers office after their Highers results, but in Scotland it does not operate under the title of AFEIS.

You will derive most benefit from your contact with school or the careers service if you have prepared yourself in advance by giving some thought to what you hope to gain from the interview. Make a note of the points that must be discussed and of the questions that you wish to raise, and compile a list of all relevant information that you glean.

The following initial questions will serve as general guidelines:

1. How realistic is it to pursue the same direction as before?
2. If it still appears to be within the bounds of possibility what should I do now?
3. If it is clear from my self-assessment, or because my results now preclude it, that a change of emphasis is indicated, what are my options?
4. What practical steps should I now take?

5. Where will I obtain the necessary information?

A thorough discussion with a teacher or careers adviser of your personal aims, and an assessment of what has gone wrong and the conclusions to be drawn will be the foundations on which to build your future plans. A number of possible courses of action can then be presented to you and should be weighed up carefully before deciding where to target yourself.

The higher education race

Speed may be of the essence, however, if you have a course of study in mind for the coming session, as remaining vacancies are snapped up quickly. It would be a mistake though to rush headlong into any course without due consideration merely for the sake of jumping onto the higher education 'bandwagon'. If it is your intention to deviate considerably from your original plan, do pause and ponder the pros and cons. It is quite possible to investigate several options without making an immediate and irrevocable decision.

Vacancies for universities, polytechnics and colleges are published through national computerised services and should be available for consultation in careers offices and some schools and colleges. These include the Educational Counselling and Credit Transfer Information Service (ECCTIS), Prestel Education and the Times Network Systems (TTNS). (You may not find these services widely available in Scotland.)

UCCA and PCAS operate a 24 hour telephone information service which you yourself may contact on 0272 217244 (UCCA) and 0272 217721 (PCAS). Information on courses which may have vacancies and the minimum points required for consideration are available through this service, which comes into operation shortly after publication of examination results and is updated daily until the end of September. Do not expect advice to be provided, however, about any problems concerning your application – these should be referred directly to UCCA or PCAS – as they are solely intended to give vacancy information.

For details of vacancies on degree and diploma courses in colleges of higher education in the public sector telephone 01-368-1299. You can also send a written enquiry to The Observer Student

Service, Middlesex Polytechnic, Trent Park, Barnet, Hertfordshire, EN4 0PT. Napier Polytechnic of Edinburgh (031-444 2266) offers centralised information for vacancies in the Scottish Central Institutions.

Your enquiry to any of these services will be dealt with more promptly if you give clear information about the subjects in which you are interested. Universities and the other institutions need a few days to analyse results before they are in a position to publicise vacancies, so allow a short time to elapse before making contact.

'Clearing' is a term familiar to most students. It is the system whereby last minute vacancies are filled after results are announced, and although you may think that it bears a resemblance to a cattle market it could prove to be your salvation. It does in fact succeed in placing a good proportion of those who aspire to higher education onto courses. If you have sufficient passes to be eligible you will automatically receive clearing information, so long as you have already submitted an application. UCCA, PCAS and CRCH (the Central Register and Clearing House) are notified by universities, polytechnics and those colleges which operate a centralised system of any unfilled vacancies. Applicants have the opportunity to indicate an interest in up to four courses from which will be selected the most appropriate.

It is, however, inadvisable to sit back and await developments as you will find that others will have pre-empted the best remaining places. So, if you want to be in with a chance get out into the market place and shop around. Clearing operates on a 'first come first served' basis and institutions are prepared to accept direct communication from students, but it does pay to plan your strategy. Select only the courses for which you appear to have some likelihood of success and do not waste time on speculative applications where you have no chance of acceptance. It does not follow that you will secure a place just because you have the minimum points that are acceptable, as other factors are taken into consideration by the selectors.

Once you have established where there are places still to be filled make a short list of those that meet your requirements, and if possible have a number of alternatives 'up your sleeve'. If you have the opportunity to study prospectuses – perhaps using the careers service or a good public reference library – before proceeding to make contact you will avoid wasting your time applying for inappropriate courses at unsuitable places. Oxford and Cambridge never accept candidates through Clearing and some other universities, notably Bristol and Durham, show little enthusiasm for the clearing candidate. Some institutions also show preference to previous applicants, as they have shown commitment to them.

The direct approach

With your short list of suitable places in order of preference in front of you, start to make contact by telephone with admissions tutors. Steel yourself for the inevitable frustrations of telephone communication at a peak time when everyone is understandably under pressure. Ask to speak to the admissions tutor for the subject in which you are interested. It is important to find out his or her name and extension number in case you cannot be put through in the first instance, or in case you are cut off before the switchboard connects you with the department concerned, and so that you get to speak to the right person if you have to call again. Be prepared to make more than one call to the same institution before tracking down the person to whom you need to speak, and do not let yourself be easily discouraged. Once contact with the appropriate person has been made state your name and what you wish to discuss clearly. Be brief and to the point. Avoid forgetting essential questions by having a written note of them in front of you along with any details relevant to your application such as your UCCA, PCAS or CRCH number.

You could even apply in person to a local institution by presenting yourself at their general enquiry desk. A polite and determined student can sometimes cut through some of the bureaucracy involved. Whatever your method of approach, it is bound to be time-consuming, and you will have to work at it with determination. A sympathetic teacher or careers adviser who has time to devote to your case might be prepared to take some of the burden from your shoulders and could also speak up on your behalf.

If, after all your efforts, interest is shown in your application there will be standard procedures which you must follow, and you should check the requirements with the admissions tutor concerned. Universities and polytechnics operate what is referred to as the 'Q'

Procedure, and you should receive full details of this on receipt of Clearing information. Briefly, if a university or polytechnic shows interest in receiving an application from you through Clearing and you have been informed that a 'Q' request will be submitted by it to UCCA or PCAS, this means that your application form will be requested for scrutiny. You should then name that institution as the first choice on your Clearing entry form. You are advised not to obtain 'Q' requests from more than one university or polytechnic at a time as to do so may delay referral of your application to your preferred institution. Although a 'Q' request does not guarantee a place, it is hopeful.

Automatic referral

Should you not manage to obtain a 'Q' request, complete your Clearing application with as realistic choices as possible. Applicants for over-subscribed courses who are inflexible about location or whose examination grades are low will be likely to find difficulty in obtaining a place.

Advertisements abound to attract students such as you. You will find extensive press coverage in the pre- and post-examination 'blues' period. *The Guardian, The Independent, The Observer, The Daily Telegraph* and *Sunday Telegraph* and *The Times* and *The Sunday Times* often run series of articles dealing with the dilemma faced by so many students at this time, and they can be useful sources of information. It is worth visiting your local reference library regularly to scan them for any items appropriate to your needs.

Advertisements for courses proliferate and they are offered at a wide variety of academic seats of learning. Universities, polytechnics and colleges whose quotas have not been filled vie with each other to attract students as yet unplaced. Colleges offering retakes promote the benefits to be derived from studying at their establishments, in glowing terms. Every conceivable type of course advertises its wares to you, the prospective consumer, and at this time of year watch out too for phone-in radio programmes which devote air space to question and answer sessions on the topic of the post-examination dilemma.

Employers and professions

Higher Education may not of course have featured in your plans in the first place. A company training scheme or direct entry into a profession with the intention of study for professional qualifications on a part-time day or evening basis could well have been your original choice. Although lack of the appropriate qualification could now bar you from entry to your chosen profession or company training scheme, you should still make contact to discuss the position before assuming that all is lost. Some employers may be flexible and still keep their offer open. Be guided by their advice as regards the feasibility of following the career of your choice, for, if their requirements for particular subjects in which you have not succeeded are directly related to the job, it could indicate that you are following the wrong path. It would, for instance, be ill-advised to contemplate a future in medical laboratory science without sound scientific ability. You should seek guidance on alternative professional or company training schemes from your careers service or from the professional body concerned.

Trawling for information

Do not underestimate the help that might be at hand from family and friends, though keep an open mind about suggestions from that quarter. Tap the resources available to you, for by casting your net widely you will draw in a valuable trawl. Older brothers and sisters and friends who have suffered in a similar way with disappointing results and have come through smiling can also give you the benefit of their experience. At the end of the day, however, it will be *your* decision as to what use you make of the advice acquired from all these sources.

Your route ahead may as yet be unclear but your 'fact-finding mission' should provide the 'maps' from which to chart your course. Make a reconnaissance, therefore, of each possible direction by studying the options.

What are the options?

Having taken some positive steps you should now be aware that there is a glimmer of light at the end of the tunnel which, on closer inspection, reveals a kaleidoscope of options. Four main areas of possibility emerge. Whether the opportunity to pursue your original plan still exists, or whether a complete change of direction is now indicated you would do well to explore these options before taking any decision. It is worth widening your horizons by considering the alternatives. Bear in mind that even if you still hope for success in the area of your first choice, it is not guaranteed, and a radical rethink may yet be required.

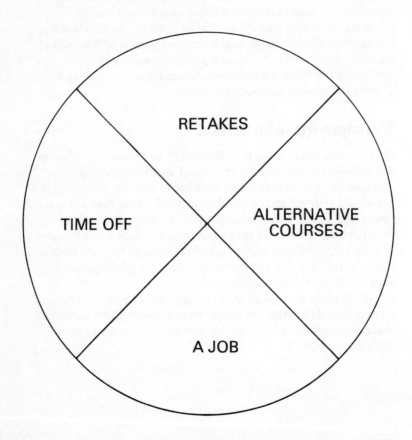

The better your qualifications in A-levels or Highers, the wider will be your choice of courses and careers. On this basis it could, therefore, be worth improving your grades by retaking one or more subjects.

Alternative courses

If, however, the prospect of retracing your steps is daunting, there is no shortage of alternative courses, some of whose academic requirements may be less stringent than those previously required of you. It could still be within the bounds of possibility to study your chosen subject at a different type of institution. A viable alternative to a university degree (if you have sufficient passes to matriculate) could be a degree at a polytechnic, a college of higher education, or a Scottish central institution. They offer a wide range of courses of both an academic and vocational nature, and the opportunity to study modular degrees or follow 'sandwich' courses. As entry requirements for certain subjects at university are higher than for others, it could also be worth investigating the possibility of acceptance onto a course where competition is not so stiff.

A Diploma of Higher Education could also be considered. (A DipHE – which is not available in Scotland – is a two year course which may be compared to the first two years of a degree course. Students usually transfer to an appropriate degree course with two years credit.)

Insufficient qualifications may, however, preclude a degree course at this stage and you might like to consider a diploma. The Business and Technician Education Council (BTEC) and the equivalent Scottish Vocational Education Council (SCOTVEC) provide a variety of courses and cover subjects as wide-ranging as art and design, catering, and information technology. They aim to prepare students for jobs in commerce and industry and are acceptable qualifications in all parts of the country. A Higher National Diploma (HND) is a two year course and it is sometimes possible for students to transfer to a degree course if they do well in their first year. Entry qualifications for these courses are lower than for degree courses.

A multitude of job-related courses are available for the awards of examining bodies such as the Royal Society of Arts (RSA), (which include secretarial and office skills and computing), and City and Guilds of London Institute (CGLI) which covers over 200 subjects ranging from community care to engineering. There are also many courses run by professional bodies; by regional examining boards, and by individual colleges. As you can see the number of different options can be confusing and it is as well to consider one aspect at a time. There is plenty of information to assist you, and once more you can use the resources of your local careers office or a well-stocked public library as a starting point. An initial reference guide to courses throughout the U.K. is CRAC's *Directory of Further Education.*

Alternatively you can acquire a nucleus of information at very little cost by making a few telephone calls. The Council for National Academic Awards (CNAA) produces a free publication entitled *Directory of First Degree and Diploma of Higher Education Courses* which gives a resumé of all such courses throughout the U.K. Professional bodies (who can be found in the telephone directory) usually publish free leaflets with detailed information about entry requirements.

The scope of courses in your local area is readily obtainable by making direct contact by telephone or in person with colleges in your vicinity.

Or employment . . .

Employment, with its prospect of independence and a wage, may appear to be an attractive proposition. Job opportunities do vary of course in different parts of the country, and in some areas it will be a more realistic option than in others. Your local Jobcentre will be a starting point for vacancies. It makes sense to look for a job that offers prospects rather than one which may have superficial attractions but could lead you into a dead end. Above all, look for a job which offers training leading towards a nationally-recognised qualification. Many large organisations have their own training schemes providing a programme of work experience, training, and education at college. Smaller firms too may encourage their employees to gain a qualification relevant to their business by giving the opportunity for time off work to attend day release or block release courses at a local college.

Self-employment may be your ultimate goal and with a strong entrepreneurial streak you could make a great success of it. The Prince's Youth Business Trust, 8 Jockey's Fields, London, WC1R 4TJ (Tel. 01-831 0313) helps 18–25 year olds who wish to set up on their own.

Time off

Taking time off if you have had enough of study presents a refreshing prospect. A break now could give you the chance to reappraise your situation and may help you see your path ahead more clearly. You would thus avoid the pitfall of a hasty decision. If you put your time to good use and don't look on it as a fallow year it could be an exciting option. For an idea of what time out can involve, read *Taking A Year Off* from Trotman and Company Ltd.

Working it out

There are clearly a number of factors for you to weigh up before reaching a conclusion. Gather as much information as possible from the sources outlined below and in the following chapters, and study each carefully. As you rotate your kaleidoscope of options, pause to absorb and reflect on the pattern it presents before reaching your conclusion.

Business and Technician Education Council (BTEC)
Central House,
Upper Woburn Place,
London WC1H 0HH   (Tel. 01-388 3288)

Scottish Vocational Education Council (SCOTVEC)
Hanover House,
24 Douglas Street,
Glasgow G2 7NQ,
Scotland   (Tel. 041-248 7900)

30

Disappointing results

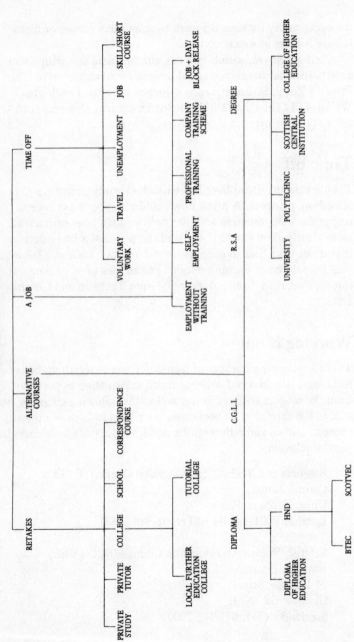

Royal Society of Arts (RSA)
8 John Adam Street,
London WC2N 6EZ   (Tel. 01-930 5115)

City and Guilds of London Institute (CGLI)
76 Portland Place,
London W1N 4AA   (Tel. 01-580 3050)

The Council for National Academic Awards (CNAA)
344-354 Gray's Inn Road,
London WC1X 8BP   (Tel. 01-278 4411)

Are retakes worth it?

Most students do not relish the prospect of retakes. To go back on your tracks has little appeal particularly when you have been looking forward to foraging ahead into the adult world with its taste of independence and spice of new friendships. Any delay is irksome and to wait another year can seem an eternity. A bit like a mountaineer, you have toiled up the foothills and scaled the heights, only to discover that instead of being at the summit yet another peak lies ahead. It's very disheartening. To summon strength for the final assault can seem daunting and yet, having reached this point, it could be better to go on than to retreat. However much you may have thought that you could not bear to go through it all again, do be prepared to change your mind – but only if it appears *right* to retake. The crux of the matter is whether or not it is the correct decision for *you*, and this will depend on a number of factors.

Consider the following questions:–

Have I the ability to improve on my results?

There is little point in spending up to a year on retaking subjects for which you have little aptitude. A frank discussion with your teachers would be a guide to your abilities in subjects where results are unsatisfactory. You should certainly try to clarify whether, given time and tuition your performance is likely to improve. If it transpires that your ability in a certain subject is modest, and little improvement can be expected then you are probably wasting your time in retaking it. Should it appear that you have a good chance of success, with more study, it could be worthwhile considering retaking one or more subjects.

Often entry into a course stipulates a particular grade in a subject and you may therefore feel compelled to retake to reach that target. *Stop and think before rushing into this*, as even if it is not your specialist subject it may indicate that you are likely to use it on your course. If you have experienced difficulty in it at *this* stage it could indicate that you are on the wrong track and need a change of direction. Admissions tutors too take a dim view of poor results in subjects which are essential for the success of their courses.

Should I consider introducing a new subject or subjects at this stage in the hope that I will have more success?

Your original choice of subjects could have been made with a certain career in mind which after your self-assessment is clearly no longer viable. You could also have been persuaded to include, for instance, some science subjects to 'keep the door open' for a possible future in engineering or technology when your personal preference lay in another direction. You are not limited to the study of your old subjects and it *is* feasible to start afresh with one or two new ones. Some, such as politics, business studies or law can adequately be covered in a year. AS levels too could add another dimension. You could therefore drop a subject in which you found difficulty, so long as it is not essential, and introduce a new one. The prospect of retakes on this basis would also be less boring with the stimulus of a new field of study.

Is it really worth retaking A-levels/Highers?

Entry requirements for some courses are less demanding than for others and some employers will consider entrants whose studies have taken them up to A-level or Highers standard even if the actual results fall short of expectation. On this basis you could find a place with your present qualifications, and the following two chapters offer suggestions for alternative courses and jobs.

You might decide, however, that having set your heart on a certain course of action – going to university for instance – you do not wish to consider alternatives at this stage. But are you still likely to be offered a place on the course of your choice if you retake? In some subjects, such as medicine or law, admissions tutors are reluctant to consider students who have had to have a second 'stab' at their exams, and for most you are likely to require higher grades than for the first time applicant. You would be wise to check the situation before assuming that retakes will be acceptable. Test the water by starting with those places where you had offers whose requirements you have been unable to meet. It is quite permissible to ring up and ask the admissions tutors if they would reconsider your application for next year with retakes, and if so what grades they would expect. You will find that some tutors give an unequivocal response, while others are inclined to be non-committal, and it will not be so easy to gauge from their reply what your chances are. It is, however, fairly safe to assume that so long as you improve your grades and are applying for courses that are not highly competitive you will not be discriminated against by reason of your retakes.

Retakes for a degree? Is a degree really worth it?

This may be a good time to ask yourself *why* you want to go on to higher education if this is your intention. Is a further three or four years right for *you*?

Not everyone benefits from higher education and it is unwise to embark on it just because it is the norm in your school, in your family or among your friends. If A-levels or Highers have been an uphill struggle you might find difficulty in coping with a degree course. Before assuming that retakes and a degree is the automatic route to success ask yourself the following questions:

- Have I sufficient interest in any subject to wish to study it in depth for the next few years?
- Am I likely to be able to cope comfortably with the academic rigours of a degree course?
- Will a degree benefit me in my career?
- Am I being brainwashed by parents, teachers or friends into thinking that higher education is essential?
- Will I be able to motivate and organise myself sufficiently to study without constant supervision?
- Am I independent enough to be able to stand on my own feet if I plan to live away from home?

There are of course sound reasons for choosing to go on to Higher Education. For some careers, such as pharmacy it is essential, and for others, such as chartered accountancy, it is the norm. Many employers too recruit graduates to groom them for their senior positions and your chances of success in the company are enhanced by a degree. The demand for graduates continues to grow as many employers who would not have been in the graduate market a few years ago join what is known as the 'Milk Round'. Unemployment tends to be lower among graduates than among those with less academic qualifications, and they have access to better paid positions than most non-graduates. Mere possession of a degree is not, however, an automatic passport to a satisfying and highly paid job, and a mediocre degree with little relevance to the requirements of the job market may be less beneficial than three years in employment.

Time spent in higher education can, of course, be very fruitful from the point of view of your intellectual development and there are the positive social aspects of association with fellow students and the opportunity for independence if you live away from home.

Assessing your motives

Having mulled over these points you might find it useful to talk it through with a member of staff from your school or a careers adviser from your local careers service. Your parents too will be very much involved in your decision, and financial considerations will also have to be taken into account. Be clear in your own mind what your motives are for choosing higher education before committing yourself to several years of further study.

Retaking examinations is always a bit of a gamble. Unless there are obvious reasons for unsatisfactory results you can never be quite certain that you have the ability to improve or that you will be any better off if you introduce a new subject. Most students who retake *do* improve but not dramatically – so, don't expect miracles! It requires determination and motivation to carry you through what may not be the best time of your life.

Where shall I retake?

A decision to retake presents the problem of whether to study at your old school, at a local college of further education, or to investigate an independent college which specialises in retakes. Private study at home either on your own or with the help of a tutor is another alternative.

Not all schools are geared up to accommodate students who wish to retake. If your school is not then you will need to look elsewhere. In Scotland, where a number of students opt to stay on after Highers for a sixth year in any case and study for the Certificate of Sixth Year Studies (CSYS), it is quite usual to return to school at this stage. In other parts of the country a return to school could be unsatisfactory and may not offer the facility to retake. The advantages of returning to a school that does cater for retakes are that the teachers know your strengths and weaknesses, and you in your turn will have no delay in settling into a new environment.

Take a look at your local sixth form college or college of further education if a return to school is not 'on the cards'. Your local education authority or careers service is the first point of contact for a list of colleges. Investigate the courses that it runs by going along and asking for a prospectus or refer to one in your local library. Follow this up, if it appears to offer the classes you require, by making an appointment to discuss enrolment. It may not of course be easy to slot into a local college at this stage. The best ones may already be full or be unable to offer you the subject or combination of subjects you require.

What can you do then if neither your school nor your local college can provide the necessary assistance?

Home study

To retake examinations it is not in fact essential to go through the entire course again. You could study at home possibly working with a private tutor or by using distance learning, and apply to retake your examination at a recognised examination centre in your area. But it is not easy as this method does require a great deal of self-discipline, particularly if you do not enlist the help of a tutor. While it may be quite feasible to cope with one subject which only requires a small improvement, it is much more difficult if you're tackling more than one. You might of course find that regular private tuition will be sufficient to boost your achievement. The best source for a tutor is usually personal recommendation, for although you will find advertisements for tutors in the local press and even small advertisements in local shops you have no way of knowing how effective they will be. However well-qualified or experienced a tutor may be (and do check credentials!) unless you get on well and feel at ease with him or her you are unlikely to make good progress. Approach your school in the first instance for a tutor as there will probably be teachers there who undertake this work, or who can recommend a colleague who would be prepared to take you on. A local college too may be able to recommend tutors. The parental 'grapevine' usually works well in this area, and your parents

may have friends with sons or daughters who have required tuition
and can suggest a suitable person. The undivided attention you
receive from a private tutor is an advantage but lack of stimulus
from other students can be a disadvantage.

Correspondence courses

Private study can be supplemented by distance learning, and there
are correspondence colleges which cater for your level of study. It
is advisable to ensure that you select a reputable college whose
standards meet those laid down by the Council for the Accreditation
of Correspondence Colleges (27 Marylebone Road, London
NW1 5JS, Tel. 01-935 5391).

The following correspondence colleges are accredited by the
Council for the Accreditation of Correspondence Colleges:

The Civil Service Correspondence School
Ware, Herts.   Tel. 0920-5926
International Correspondence Schools
312 High Street, Sutton, Surrey SM1 1PR   Tel. 01-643 9568
Mercers College
Ware, Herts.   Tel. 0920-5926
National Extension College
18 Brooklands Avenue, Cambridge CB2 2HN
Tel. 0223-316644
The Rapid Results College
Tuition House, 27/37 St George's Road, London SW19 4DS
Tel. 01-947 2211
Wolsey Hall
Oxford OX2 6PR   Tel. 0865-310310

Tutorial colleges

You might consider studying at an independent tutorial college
(sometimes referred to as a 'crammer') which specialises in retakes.
Your school may have links with such a college and be able to
recommend one based on the experience of former pupils. Tutorial
colleges offer the positive benefits of small classes, intensive courses,
and flexibility. In some areas of the country, however, they are

'thin on the ground' – the majority are in the south of England.

The benefits

1. Small classes

In some cases a small independent tutorial college could be the answer to a student's plight. The student who has 'limped' along with learning difficulties, or study related problems which have lain undetected in large classes in large schools, may find that the answer to their problems lies in small classes (probably no more than eight to ten). With the very personal attention that these colleges offer there is the opportunity to 'go back to square one' if necessary with aspects of a subject that may have been a cause of long-term difficulty.

2. Intensive courses

For students who have narrowly missed reaching their target and do not plan a radical change of subject, the short intensive course of one or two terms in which tutorial colleges specialise may be sufficient to improve their grades.

Beware however of the short intensive course if you hope to see considerable improvement in poor results, or if you plan a major change of subjects. While it is tempting to try to retake in as short a time as possible in order to get it over and done with (and of course this may be essential for financial reasons), it can be counterproductive. Also, if a change of examination board is involved it could mean that in a subject such as English you could be required to study a number of new texts which would be extremely time-consuming.

It takes time to settle down in a new place and to get used to staff, different teaching methods and other students. And it is not unknown for students to come up with even worse results by rushing to retake, and this is of course very demoralising.

3. Flexibility

The flexibility of subjects offered by tutorial colleges is also an attraction. They do not suffer from the constraints imposed on larger schools where certain combinations of subjects cannot be accommodated on their timetable, and are therefore in a better position to tailor courses to the individual student's requirements. It is even possible to study one or two subjects over a year while retaking another after only one term's study. For some, this has the advantage of spreading the examination pressure and of allowing more time for a concentrated effort on a new subject or one that is particularly troublesome.

It is in the interests of any tutorial college to ensure that its students achieve good grades. Its reputation is built and maintained on the academic success of its students. A good college will demand a high level of commitment as far as work is concerned, and will usually expect classwork to be backed up by a considerable amount of homework. There is usually, therefore, a high level of motivation with little likelihood of distraction from disaffected students. The fact that everyone is in the same boat is likely to put your own disappointment into perspective and it is less embarrassing to 'mark time' with others similarly placed than to repeat classes with younger students in your school or local college where you will feel your failure more keenly.

The disadvantages

One major drawback about tutorial colleges is their expense, as it is unlikely that you will receive financial assistance from your local authority for such a course. This is a factor which prompts students to opt for as short a course as possible – and thus suffer as a result.

As these colleges can be costly, you and your parents will wish to be certain that you are making the correct choice if you opt for tutorial college. Many of the colleges are small and unable to offer the full range of non-academic pursuits and sports facilities to which you are accustomed in a larger school. By their very nature they encourage you to concentrate on the academic aspect, to the exclusion of other distractions. While this serves its purpose, you may have to be prepared to forego your favourite sport for instance for the duration of retakes. It is worth remembering that your local further education college is more likely to offer similar extra curricular activity to your school than a tutorial college.

How can you be sure that an independent college in which you are interested is in fact a reputable establishment? It is all too easy to be persuaded of their merits by glossy college prospectuses, but it pays to look at a few before making your decision. If possible, try to have a recommendation either from school or a student whom you know to have emerged from one of its courses successfully. Beware of the establishment which appears eager to accept you with the glowing promise of boosting your results. Ask for firm evidence of its success rate with previous students as this is the criterion by which it will eventually be judged. Expect to be grilled yourself as to your potential, before acceptance. Check the facilities including library and quiet study areas, and laboratories if you require them.

A reliable check of standards is if the college is accredited by the British Accreditation Council for Independent Further and Higher Education (BAC), Middlesex Polytechnic, Bounds Green Road, London, N11 2NQ (Tel. 01-368 1299 Ext. 7399) and if it is a member of the Conference for Independent Further Education (CIFE), Lovehayne Farm, Southleigh, Colyton, Devon, EX13 6JE (Tel. 0404-87 241). These bodies were established to improve and enhance standards offered by such colleges and to ensure regular inspection. CIFE operates a special 'Hot line' to advise on its colleges in August and September (Hot line number – Tel. 01-823 7443).

The following colleges outside London are accredited by BAC

Basil Paterson College (CIFE)
22 Abercromby Place, Edinburgh EH3 6QE   031-556 7695

Bosworth Tutors (CIFE)
9–11 St George's Avenue, Northampton NN2 6JA   0604-719988

Brooke House VIth Form College (CIFE)
Market Harborough, Leicestershire LE16 7AU   0858-62452

Brown and Brown Tutorial College (CIFE)
20 Warnborough Road, Oxford OX2 6JA   0865-56311

Cambridge Centre for Sixth-Form Studies (CIFE)
1 Salisbury Villas, Station Road, Cambridge CB1 2JF   0223-316890

Cambridge Seminars (CIFE)
4 Hawthorn Way, Cambridge CB4 1AX   0223-313464

Cherwell Tutors (CIFE)
Greyfriars, Paradise Street, Oxford OX1 1LD   0865-242670

Concord College (CIFE)
Acton Burnell Hall, Shrewsbury, Shropshire SY5 7PF   06944-631

Connaught College (CIFE)
Westgate Buildings, Bath, Avon BA1 1EB   0225-63491

Davies's College
44 Cromwell Road, Hove, East Sussex BN3 3ER   0273-723911

Educare College (CIFE)
Saintaidd, Burnage Lane, Manchester M19 1DR   061-442 0858

Edward Greene Tutorial Establishment
45 Pembroke Street, Oxford OX1 1BP   0865-248308

Hurtwood House (CIFE)
Holmbury St Mary, Near Dorking, Surrey RH5 6NU
0483-277416

Irwin Academy (CIFE)
164 London Road, Leicester LE2 1ND   0533-552648

Kirby Lodge (CIFE)
Little Shelford, Cambridge CB2 5ES   0223-842069

Mander Portman Woodward, Birmingham (CIFE)
38 Highfield Road, Edgbaston, Birmingham, B15 3ED
021-454 9637

Padworth College (CIFE)
Near Reading, Berkshire RG7 4NP   073529-2644/5

St Aldates College (CIFE)
Rose Place, St Aldates, Oxford OX1 1SB   0865-240111

St Giles College (CIFE)
Silverdale Road, Eastbourne, East Sussex BN20 7AJ
0323-29167/641502

St Joseph's Hall (CIFE)
Junction Road, Oxford OX4 2UJ   0865-711829

Stafford House Tutorial College (CIFE)
68 New Dover Road, Canterbury, Kent CT1 3EQ   0277-453237/8/9

Wallace Tutorial College
17 Dublin Street, Edinburgh EH1 3PG   031-556 3634

Wolsey Hall Tutorial College
66 Banbury Road, Oxford OX2 6PR   0865-52200

The following Colleges in the London area are accredited by BAC

Albany College (CIFE)
23–24 Queens Road, London NW4 2TL   01-202 5965/9748

Cambridge Tutors College (CIFE)
Water Tower Hill, Croydon, Surrey CR0 5SX   01-668 5284

Capital College
Red Lion House, 47 Red Lion Street, London WC1R 4PF
01-404 5883

Collingham Tutors (CIFE)
23 Collingham Gardens, London SW5 0HL   01-370 6739

David Game Tutorial College (CIFE)
86 Old Brompton Road, London SW7 3LQ   01-584 9097/7580

Davies's College (CIFE)
66 Southampton Row, London WC1B 4BY   01-405 2933

Davies, Laing & Dick (CIFE)
10 Pembridge Square, London W2 4ED   01-727 2797

Duff-Miller Tutorial College (CIFE)
59 Queen's Gate, London SW7 5JW 01-225 0577/8/9

Fine Art Tutors (CIFE)
85 Belsize Park Gardens, London NW3 4NJ   01-586 0312
(GCE A-level specialising in the Arts)

Lansdowne Independent Sixth-Form College (CIFE)
7–9 Palace Gate, London W8 5LS   01-581 3307/8

Mander Portman Woodward, London (CIFE)
5 Wetherby Place, London SW7 4NX   01-373 6251

Milestone Tutorial College (CIFE)
85 Cromwell Road, London SW7 5BW   01-373 4956/7

Modern Tutorial College (CIFE)
21 Kilburn Lane, London W10 4AA   01-960 5899

A useful contact for guidance about educational courses in the independent sector is Gabbitas, Truman and Thring Educational Trust, Broughton House, 6–8 Sackville Street, Piccadilly, London W1X 2BR (Tel. 01-734 0161/01-439 2071).

To help determine the right college for you use this checklist of useful questions:–

1. Can they offer the subject or combination of subjects that I require in the time that I want?
2. Will I have to study for a different examining board?
3. What size are the classes?
4. What are the likely numbers of students studying the same subjects as me?
5. What has been the success rate of previous students?
6. Have students gone on to the type of place on which I have set my sights?
7. Is the college accredited by BAC and a member of CIFE?
8. What facilities does it offer?
9. What are the fees and are there any hidden extras?
10. Is accommodation provided or assistance given if I intend living away from home?

Check the credentials of its staff by looking at its staff list in the prospectus or by asking to see it.

Part time study

Financial considerations can preclude full time study for retakes and it may be necessary for you to take a job and study part-time. This can be very demanding and taxing, but it is of course a method which was quite common in previous generations. If you do not need to improve your grades by a great deal this could be an option, but it will be more demanding if you require considerable improvement.

Weighing it up

Clearly there are many factors to be considered about the different options for retakes, and unfortunately you probably don't have a great deal of time to ponder these points. A glance at the following

chart which outlines the pros and cons should help you work out
the best option for *you*.

RETAKES AT SCHOOL		RETAKES AT LOCAL 6TH FORM OR FURTHER EDUCATION COLLEGE	
PROS	CONS	PROS	CONS
1. Your strengths and weaknesses are known	1. Might not offer facility to retake	1. Offers similar facilities to school	1. Takes time to get used to new methods and teachers
2. You know the staff	2. Can be embarrassing to repeat classes with younger students	2. Environment is more adult than school	2. May have change of examining board
3. No change of examining board	3. Can be boring to go over the same ground in the same environment	3. Challenge of new place	3. May be required to pay fees
4. You do not require time to settle			4. May not offer the course required
5. Full facilities available			5. Not all students are motivated

PRIVATE STUDY WITH OR WITHOUT A TUTOR		TUTORIAL COLLEGES	
PROS	CONS	PROS	CONS
1. Relatively inexpensive	1. Isolation of private study	1. Small classes and personal attention	1. Takes time to get used to new methods and teachers
2. Can take a job at the same time	2. No other students to compare ideas	2. Intensive courses	2. May have a change of examining board

PRIVATE STUDY WITH OR WITHOUT A TUTOR		TUTORIAL COLLEGES	
PROS	CONS	PROS	CONS
3. Can concentrate on areas of special needs	3. Need to be highly motivated & self-disciplined	3. Flexibility	3. Expensive
	4. No one to encourage unless you have a private tutor	4. Encouragement to channel all one's energies into work	4. Limited availability depending on area of the country
		5. Other students in the same position as yourself	5. Limited extra curricular activities
			6. Facilities are likely to be less extensive than at school

James

Although I had not expected to achieve high grades in two of my A-level subjects I felt numb when I learned that I had an E in economics. With my other results – B in history and E in Latin – I would not be able to ensure a university place to read history.

Before receiving this news I thought that I could not bear to consider retakes, but faced with the situation I could no longer reject this possibility. I was encouraged by my family and my school tutor to believe that my history result showed I had the ability to succeed in a history degree at university – if only I could improve in my other subjects to gain a place. I considered the usual options, such as studying at a polytechnic – where I had in fact the firm offer of a place – or applying for a company training scheme or a job, but rejected these in favour of retakes.

Latin was always a difficult subject for me and I did not think that there was much to be gained by retaking it, but I was optimistic about an improvement in economics. In retrospect my choice of A-level Latin and economics was probably ill-advised. At school I had been discouraged from studying politics, in which I was interested, and I decided to take the opportunity of studying this new subject if I could to avoid the boredom of repetition.

My aim was to get the exams over as soon as possible and to use the rest of my enforced year out for more interesting projects. Having seen their advertisements in newspapers, I contacted a couple of tutorial colleges and chose the one whose staff and students appeared to be most pleasant. I arranged to retake economics in November and to take politics A-level in January.

Life at tutorial college seemed more akin to university than to school with its very informal small groups of students and plenty of opportunity for discussion. It came as a surprise to me – university having been the accepted goal for the majority of my contemporaries – to discover that most of the students there had set their sights on polytechnics and I was one of the few applying to university.

I have to admit that when the time came to fill in my UCCA form yet again, I did feel that I was wasting a year of my life. The head of the college was, however, most helpful in suggesting universities which had not been mentioned by my school tutor, and from whom I subsequently received invitations to interview. Looking back I think that my original choice was influenced by my school's attitude to the prestige accorded (in their eyes) to certain universities.

My decision to retake economics in November proved to be a mistake. Although the examination board was the same as before, there really was not adequate time to cover all the topics required and as a result I failed completely. This was a bitter blow and was certainly the most difficult time for me.

At that point I was holding two offers, one of which was BCC at Royal Holloway. The other was an offer from Bangor who would accept me if I could attain C in politics. My politics result was due in March. It was a D. Certain that it was a hopeless situation I wrote to Bangor who, to my surprise, asked me for interview, and made me an offer of a place. I was in a dilemma as I was still keen on my first choice and had been discussing with my tutor the possibility of retaking yet again in June.

During the Easter holidays I mulled over the problem and decided to accept the place at Bangor. Staff and students that I had met there seemed friendly and its location on the edge of Snowdonia would offer me the opportunity of the outdoor activities that I enjoy. It was a great relief to feel that at last my future was decided.

A spell in France in the summer brushing up my French and a trip around Europe have meant that my year out has had its positive aspects. I am much better prepared now for further study than I would have been directly after school, and now I feel more confident – in fact very optimistic – about my future at university.

Alternative courses

Retakes may not be feasible for you or may hold no appeal, and yet you are still keen to proceed to higher education. Had you thought about an alternative course?

When you start to 'window shop' around, you may well be pleasantly surprised by what is on offer. However, the places available on these courses, in the aftermath of results, will not be as many as at the beginning of the 'season' and you will have to be quick off the mark if you hope to snap up the best of what remains. As with 'sale goods' though, it will be no bargain if it is not what you want. So, try to establish your requirements before you 'go shopping' for alternative courses and you will be less likely to be persuaded into a 'spur of the moment' decision which you regret later.

You should establish the following:

1. What to study
2. The level of study
3. Where to study
4. How to secure a place

What to study

What are the alternatives if you did not get the right grades for a university place? It could still be possible to study your original subject at degree or diploma level with your present qualifications at another higher education establishment. There may be a different emphasis to the subject – a course in modern languages for instance in a polytechnic or college is likely to have a much more practical application than a university course with a high literary content.

Combined studies and modular degrees

Your chosen subject could also be found in combination with another, or even with several, subjects – there is a flexibility about many polytechnic and college courses where combined studies and modular degrees are a feature. This makes for varied and interesting courses with a wide range of modules from which to chose. Modular courses are usually based on a central core of common subjects and

offer scope also for the study of less closely related subjects. For
the student who is uncertain of where his or her true interests lie,
or who finds variety more appealing than the in-depth study of a
single subject such courses have a strong appeal. Once you have
perused one or two of the handbooks of courses you may even
abandon your original subject in favour of a more interesting and
exciting alternative.

Change of course, change of career goal

Take care though! Don't opt for superficially attractive alternatives
without weighing up the pros and cons. It is always important to
investigate *where* a course is likely to lead. Is it vocationally
orientated? Try to find out what past students have gone on to do
on completion. Bear in mind too that you will be asked to justify
your choice of subjects and show an informed interest if invited
for interview, and on this count alone you should be as
knowledgeable as possible. A change of course may indicate a
change of career goal. Ask yourself if this is what you want.

The level of study

The next consideration after your subject choice is the level of
qualification at which you intend to set your sights. Having studied
to A-level or Highers standard you will be most likely to choose
between a degree, a Diploma of Higher Education (DipHE), a
BTEC or SCOTVEC Higher National Diploma, or another
professional qualification. Both the DipHE and Higher National
Diploma are recognised on their own merits and can also be used
as qualifications from which to proceed to degree courses.
Sometimes these courses overlap with the first two years of a degree
course and a transfer can be arranged. It is however inadvisable to
assume that it will be possible to transfer, and it is wiser to embark
on such a course only if you are convinced of its value.

The two year DipHE, which was originally intended for
prospective teachers now caters for a broader range of study but it
is often used as a starter course with a view to an eventual degree.

BTEC and SCOTVEC HND and HNC courses are highly
flexible programmes of courses which are designed in 'building
blocks'. They are vocational and qualify you to work in certain

areas of work, for example scientific laboratories, agriculture, art, business and so on. What you learn on these courses is directly related to the certain types of work. You thus need to be quite sure about your career goals if you opt for a BTEC or SCOTVEC course.

The BTEC and SCOTVEC courses consist of core studies and work experience plus a variety of optional units which are devised by the individual polytechnics, colleges and Scottish central institutions which are offering them. Because of this variety, a BTEC Higher National course (HNC or HND) in, say, business studies may be very different in content at two different colleges. You are advised to check very carefully in prospectuses and course leaflets just what is on offer. You may have to 'shop around' to find the right course for you.

For a really practical course with minimal entrance requirements the City and Guilds of London Institute (CGLI) offers a broad range of qualifications widely recognised in industry. City and Guilds provides qualifications for over half a million people every year – and the range of subjects is huge, over 300 technical subjects in all. And City and Guilds courses do have the great advantage of being available at a very large number of centres – over 2,000 – and by a range of methods of study, full time and part time. The full time courses are usually of one year's duration (but there are some two year courses at certain colleges which offer two City and Guilds certificates, one each year). And if you imagined that City and Guilds courses were only craft courses in a limited number of careers, think again. They range from travel, tourism and recreation to engineering, from professional and scientific services and chemicals and metallurgy to personal services and community care. Read the prospectus of your local college, it will tell you what is available. For the student with ambitions to enter the world of commerce the Royal Society of Arts (RSA) awards its own qualifications in office and secretarial skills and some commercial subjects. RSA courses can be taken both part-time and full-time and cover a very wide spectrum of careers – accounting, administration, languages, information technology and much much more.

Then there are Pitmans courses which are offered over a wide range of subjects in secretarial skills, office skills, retail and distribution, office technology, computing etc. These too are to be found at your local colleges of further education.

Your local college will almost certainly also offer courses leading to the awards of the LCCI – London Chamber of Commerce and Industry – in a great variety of business, management, accounting, advertising, language, secretarial and similar options.

Professional courses

Various courses serve to prepare students for the examinations of various professional bodies and offer exemption from part or all of their examinations. A decision to enter such a course indicates a particular career goal. There are different professional qualifications with differing modes of entry, details of which can be obtained from the professional institutions concerned. For some such as pharmacy and speech therapy a degree is the only recognised mode of entry, while for others such as accountancy, engineering and technology, hotel and catering management, and nursing there are qualifications at degree and diploma level. Many professions now expect degree or equivalent qualifications for potential senior management positions and will look to those with HND qualifications for their junior management and upper technical level jobs.

A professional course is likely by its very nature to channel you into a specific area where academic ability alone may not suffice. For example, there must be evidence of concern for patients and physical stamina to be successful as a student on a physiotherapy, radiography or nursing course.

The professional institutions lay down regulations for academic standards and practical experience. Some, such as the Institute of Chartered Secretaries and Administrators and the Institute of Bankers hold their own examinations. Others, such as the Royal Institute of Chartered Surveyors accept higher education qualifications such as degrees, which give exemption from the written parts of the RICS entrance qualifications.

Art and design courses

Perhaps you have a flair for art and design but you think that your academic achievement debars your entry to a degree level course at art school or polytechnic. Your talents could be directed to an HND course where your practical creativity could be developed.

But it is unlikely you could have begun a degree course straight away in any case. A year's Foundation Course is often expected of the prospective art student and for entry to a Foundation Course A-level passes may not be necessary if you have the minimum of five GCSEs at grade C or above. During a Foundation Course there is the opportunity to try out a wide range of artistic specialisation – fine art, graphic design, three dimensional design, textiles or fashion. If you successfully complete your foundation course, you can then go on to a degree. The Art and Design Admissions Registry (ADAR) operates a centralised admissions procedure, details of which should be available at your school or local art college. For art colleges which do not participate in this scheme you should make direct application to the college of your choice.

Where to study

There is great variety in our education system and further education is by no means restricted to the universities, polytechnics or central institutions. In most parts of the country there will be a local college – there is probably one in your own area – which historically concentrated on specialised subjects usually directly related to the local industry, such as ceramics in Stafford, fishing studies in Humberside, metallurgy in Sheffield, nautical studies in Plymouth and textiles in the Borders. While there are, of course, many colleges which still specialise – in such courses as agriculture, art and design, catering, engineering and technology, music and the performing arts – other technical colleges, while still essentially vocational, have expanded their range of subjects. Your local college is therefore worth considering – its courses may be quite wide ranging.

Don't overlook the importance of *where* you choose to study in your rush to accept a place. While the subject will usually be the first consideration in any choice, the actual place where you will spend the next few years of your life is also of some importance. Even if you are not left with a wide choice at this stage try to make it as satisfactory as possible. Most institutions offer adequate sports and social facilities, but if you are a lover of the great outdoors you would clearly be better placed at a college which is at least within easy reach of the wide open spaces, rather than in an urban environment where a major expedition is required to reach the countryside.

Although you may have hoped to study away from home, you could find that your new choice of course is particularly well catered for in your own area, and it would therefore make sense to remain there. If, however, your intention had been to remain in your home town so that you could keep contact with local friends, that door may now be closed and you may have to adjust to the idea of a change of location. When selecting a new place of study take care to read prospectuses carefully so that you are aware not only of the course content but of tutorial and teaching systems, laboratory, library and residential facilities.

How to secure a place

If you have already applied for courses other than at university you will automatically be eligible for a place in their Clearing systems and will receive the necessary information. Point 3 gives guidance on how to deal with Clearing and locate vacancies.

Perhaps you have not already entered the centralised systems for a polytechnic or college place and would now like to do so. Your contact for a polytechnic place and for some colleges is the Polytechnics Central Admissions System (PCAS) PO Box 67, Cheltenham, Gloucestershire GL50 3AP (Tel. 0242 526 225), and for teacher training courses and courses in Institutes and Colleges of Higher Education your contact is Central Register and Clearing House (CRCH) 3 Crawford Place, London W1H 1BN (no telephone number is publicised). (Applications for 14 colleges of higher education whose courses are validated by universities are now made through UCCA.) For Scottish Central Institutions and colleges with no centralised system separate applications must be made.

Students in the Clearing System sometimes find that they receive offers from polytechnics or colleges to which they have made no application. This is the result of computerised systems which link vacancies to candidates by reason of their qualifications. Such offers take no account of your personal preferences and to accept one may therefore be a last resort.

Study in the U.S.A.

Students looking for a broader type of education than is offered by our university system and whose qualifications fall short of those required for university entry are sometimes attracted by the prospect of study in the U.S.A. The number of degree-awarding institutions and the range of courses is, however, extremely bewildering, and specific guidance is needed. American universities base their admission procedures on aptitude and achievement tests as well as school attainments and reports. The most selective institutions will require A-levels or Highers for which you may receive credits, but there are others where lesser qualifications are acceptable. Overseas students are usually required to take the Scholastic Aptitude Test (SAT). These tests can be taken in the U.K. at different periods of the year in various locations and sample tests are available. If it had crossed your mind that you might like to study in the U.S.A. you should contact the U.S./U.K. Educational Commission, 6 Porter Street, London W1M 2HR (Tel. 01-486 1098).

NB It is always important before embarking on a degree abroad to consider its validity in the eyes of a prospective employer in this country, as, particularly in a professional context, it may not be recognised. And remember you will have to find the money for your fares, fees and upkeep.

Weighing up the options

Before you decide on an alternative course of study you should assess the advantages and disadvantages.

Advantages

If you are accepted you can start your higher education at the same time as you originally planned, and if you stick to the same subject at the same level with only a change of institution you will feel that your results have not blown you too far 'off course'. Should you decide on a change of subject, or to study at a different level such as an HND rather than a degree it could in fact turn out to be more suited to your capabilities, and in the long run may prove to be a more realistic and satisfactory choice. A BTEC or SCOTVEC qualification in a vocational subject may in fact offer better job prospects too than a modest degree obtained at an obscure college.

Disadvantages

The same subject at a different institution may not offer the same recognition. Broadly speaking, a degree at the same level in an 'academic' subject such as history, obtained at a university is likely to have more 'currency' in the employment market than a non-university degree. This is by no means the case though in all subjects. Courses such as business studies, or engineering and technological subjects with a sandwich element studied at a polytechnic or central institution are highly regarded by employers as giving evidence of the practical ability and experience better fitted to the world of work than theoretical study.

If you opt for a lesser qualification than originally intended you could feel that you have been 'short-changed' unless you are ready to face up to the reality that it is more in line with your abilities.

One point which should not be overlooked is the question of a grant. Although you may have been eligible for a grant for your original course it is not automatically transferrable. You should check with your local authority that your alternative course is a 'designated' course which entitles you to a grant. Some local authorities are loath to make awards for certain higher education courses at colleges in another area when their local college offers the same course. Financial considerations could therefore limit your choice of location.

And finally

Bear in mind when choosing an alternative course that you need to be convinced of its validity to enjoy the experience of Higher Education. A sense of pride too, both in the course of study and the institution is important, if it is to bring you satisfaction both as a student and in the years to come.

Anne

"I'd always enjoyed being with animals. And living in the country, we were surrounded by dogs, bantams, heifers and ducks."

Anne's best subjects at school were the sciences and it seemed natural that her A-level options should be biology, chemistry and physics, originally with the intention of becoming a vet. *"With so many pets and farm animals around I had plenty of contact with the local veterinary practice. I dearly wanted to be a vet and my parents encouraged me in my ambition. But the careers teacher at school pointed out just how very stiff the competition was for places and how demanding the universities were when it came to grades."*

At first Anne could not be convinced that her ambition was unrealistic. Her parents too overestimated her abilities. But eventually she was persuaded to consider zoology as an alternative and, with offers of CCC, Anne felt her future on an interesting university course was secure.

No-one became concerned when Anne's internal school examination results in the lower sixth were disappointing. *"I'd been unwell at the time and everyone put the indifferent marks down to illness. But, looking back at it now, I should have seen the warning lights."* The school, which is an all girls establishment, has a good record in arts subjects but the number of students in the sixth form taking science subjects is not large. Compared to the rest of the group, Anne was good – and in chemistry, very good – but when compared with the student population as a whole, she was not such an outstanding candidate.

Having set her sights lower, Anne felt that the pressure on her had been eased. *"And, I'll admit, I eased up in my studies too. I'd always been a keen musician and in the school orchestra, and my ambition to get higher and higher grades at flute and piano, took more of my time. I suppose, therefore, that the A-level results when they came should not have been a surprise . . . B in chemistry, D in biology and D in physics."*

"Clearing proved to be my salvation. I began a rapid reappraisal of my future, to start with I questioned just what I was going to do with a degree in zoology anyway. I started to look for other options working with animals and in the vacancy lists I was struck that there were opportunities in agriculture, which also seemed to be a more practical solution from an employment point of view too. As a farmer's daughter I knew more than most about farming to begin with."

On the advice of her careers teacher, Anne phoned the admissions tutors in three likely universities and one seemed quite hopeful. *"I placed them first on the Clearing form and within a couple of days I had an offer, which is why I am here in Wales studying plant diseases, grasslands and farm animals rather than in Scotland setting about becoming a vet as I'd first intended."*

What about a job?

Academic life doesn't appeal to everyone. It is not unusual to find that a young person, whose A-levels have been disappointing, blossoms once away from school and out in 'the real world'. Particularly for those with a practical approach to life, to opt for a job instead of further full-time study can bring a sense of purpose which may have been previously lacking.

If you are not convinced that there is any point for you in further full-time education, a job may be the answer. It will not however be an easy option. Although there are many people who have worked their way up without the benefit of a higher education, qualifications are important. The growth of graduate recruitment among employers, the requirements of the professions for degrees and diplomas, the general level of unemployment and the expansion of the Youth Training Scheme have meant that there have been fewer suitable vacancies for school leavers who have studied A-levels or Highers. But now there *are* more vacancies, and the fact that there's a decreasing number of young people entering the job market could work in your favour.

There are jobs, and there are training schemes, but they may be limited according to the area in which you plan to work. It may not be any easier to find a job with prospects than it would be to win a place in higher education, and a decision to enter employment now will require perseverance and a positive approach on your part. Take a frank look, therefore, at your motives before deciding on this course of action, for if you view employment rather than a course as a last resort you will be unlikely to convince an employer than it is worth investing time and effort in training you.

When you decided to study for A-levels or Highers you no doubt expected that it would enhance your prospects in the job market, and it would be a mistake not to use this to your advantage by aiming for a job that offers training and prospects for your future rather than one that leads to a dead end. Many firms recruit trainees at three different levels – the school leaver with GCSEs/SCEs, the A-level or Highers entrant and the graduate. With results that may have proved inadequate for the course of your choice in higher education you may well wonder at what level you would be eligible for a company training scheme. Although, broadly speaking, entry to a training scheme mirrors entry to higher education, employers are likely to be more flexible than colleges about grades. They may even consider a candidate who has studied to this level but failed to reach the required standard, if personal attributes appear to compensate for academic deficiencies. But employers' entry requirements may be linked to those of a professional body whose examinations you would eventually be expected to take – in which case they are unlikely to be so flexible.

Your heart may sink at the mention of more examinations – it is after all quite natural to feel a strong reaction against further study after disappointing results. But if you aim for a job with training and good prospects, you are unlikely to be able to say goodbye to academic work forever. Many employers will expect their trainees to study part-time on a day release or block release basis for the professional examination relevant to their type of business, and it will certainly be to your advantage to do so, otherwise your future promotion could be blocked.

The companies and the jobs

So what are these company training schemes and how can you discover more about them? They are to be found in the public and private sectors, the Health Service, in commerce and industry, and in the world of finance. A glance at the *Job Book – The Handbook of Employment and Training for School Leavers* (CRAC) in your local library or careers service will give you a good idea of the range of employers who offer training schemes. Such a range of opportunities is not of course available in all areas of the country and unless you are prepared to move away from home you will be restricted to the jobs that are actually to be found in your own area. Your local careers service and Jobcentre will be in touch with the needs of local industry and employers and should be able to advise you about jobs with training prospects. Your school too may have links with business and industry. If you have been to an independent school which belongs to the Independent Schools Careers Organisation (ISCO) you should be able to take advantage of its careers information and appointments service.

Professional associations can sometimes give information about firms who recruit students at your level and about appropriate training schemes. The relevant professional association could be a useful point of contact if you have a specific career in mind.

Large organisations usually advertise vacancies and training schemes in the national and local press. There are specific publications which advertise opportunities – for example *Farmer's Weekly* in agriculture, and so on – and these may be found in libraries and large newsagents. Bear in mind though that many training schemes start in September and could therefore have already been advertised. So, it may be more realistic at this stage to make a direct approach to companies in your area.

Prepare a curriculum vitae (CV) giving details of your academic background, your interests and any work experience you may have had and send it with a covering letter to the recruitment manager of suitable firms. Even if they have not advertised vacancies they may be prepared to consider you. Personal contacts can also be useful. You may, for instance, have a Saturday job or have had holiday employment in a firm which could offer you permanent employment with training, or, if this is unlikely the employer may have 'an ear to the ground' and know of openings in the area. Take a look also at new companies moving into the district which may provide expansion in the local job market.

Public sector opportunities are to be found in the Civil Service, local government and the Health Service. The Civil Service, which is concerned with most aspects of national life, offers a variety of prospects. The executive grade, which leads to a future in junior management, recruits its staff from those with A-levels or Highers qualifications. There are specialist categories such as officers in Customs and Excise, the Inland Revenue and the Tax Inspectorate. Although many departments of the Civil Service are based in London there are regional offices and those of the Scottish and Welsh offices, and more Civil Service posts are being moved to the regions. Local authorities have a variety of training opportunities in their administrative and financial departments which lead to managerial positions.

The National Health Service is a large employer – the largest in Britain – and, while many of its opportunities are for those with professional qualifications such as in dietetics or occupational therapy, there are regional training schemes designed to provide managers at all levels and which combine practical on-the-job training with study for a professional qualificaton. If you have studied science subjects you may be interested in medical laboratory science where there is an entry at junior technician level.

The world of finance attracts many and there are openings in accountancy, banking, building societies and insurance companies with the prospect of professional qualifications acquired through part-time study. The ACCA qualification of the Chartered Association of Certified Accountants can be studied part-time while undergoing training in the financial departments of commercial firms, industrial firms and local authorities. Accountancy training in industry could also offer prospects of membership of the Association of Accounting Technicians or a BTEC or SCOTVEC in business studies, both as a result of day release study. The banks recruit at your level for their Management Training Schemes and expect you to pass the examinations of the Institute of Bankers for the AIB qualification. Comprehensive training schemes are also available in building societies and insurance companies with encouragement to acquire their professional qualifications.

For a more active life you could look to the police or Armed Services who invite applications from school leavers with A-levels and Highers and provide training and good prospects of promotion with the opportunity for officer entry in the Armed Services. The police force encourages entrants to take the police promotion examinations which qualify for promotion to the higher ranks.

The fast-moving world of retailing is a growth area which attracts its recruits from all levels of academic achievement, and many companies offer schemes whereby you can reach the higher echelons irrespective of scholastic ability. Chain stores, department stores, supermarkets and superstores all offer employment and well-defined training programmes for school leavers, with encouragement to study for nationally recognised retail and distribution qualifications. You would expect to be given a thorough on-the-job grounding in all aspects of the retailing operation, with training in sales techniques and merchandising, retail finance and customer relations. After appropriate experience you would be ready to move up the career ladder through supervising jobs to junior management positions. You could specialise in, for instance, department management, or merchandising or staff management.

Company training schemes with good prospects are by no

means confined to the areas mentioned above, but they are suggested as likely sources of employment as they offer prospects nationwide. Take a look in the High Street of your local town and you will see banks, building societies, insurance companies, chain stores and supermarkets. Widen your horizons by considering also other likely sources of employment in your locality. Perhaps tourism features highly in the area, and this accounts for a growing number of job opportunities and not just in the hotel and catering industry. This is an expanding area with recognised training schemes leading to the qualification of the Hotel, Catering and Institutional Management Association (HCIMA).

The subjects you have studied and your own interests will of course have a bearing on the areas to which you are attracted. For those whose interests lie in science and technology, medical laboratory science or radiography offer opportunities at your level. Then there are traineeships at technician level in the engineering industry and although entry requirements for these are GCSE/SCEs some companies operate accelerated schemes for the student who has studied A-levels or Highers. During the training period you would be expected to study for the BTEC/SCOTVEC qualifications relevant to your particular branch of engineering. Mathematical ability and a liking for outdoor work might attract you to quantity surveying, with training, on-the-job experience, and study leading to the ARICS qualification of the Royal Institute of Chartered Surveyors.

Should you aspire to a future in a design or media environment it may not be so easy to find training schemes suited to your level of attainment. Professional designers are normally expected to have taken full-time training courses. Radio, television and journalism are all highly competitive but opportunities do exist in technical and operational work, and for journalistic staff in local radio and local newspapers.

If you live in a rural area and wish to work on the land or in forestry it may be difficult to slot into a training scheme particularly geared to the school leaver with A-levels or Highers. Many young people start an Agricultural Training Board (ATB) apprenticeship or craft training schemes whose academic requirements are usually at the GCSE/SCE level. Others will enter with a degree, a BTEC or Scottish National Certificate.

These opportunities give only a flavour of what is on offer. Your local Careers Service can advise you on training schemes which relate to your aptitudes and interests.

Richard

"Four weeks before I took A-levels my parents split up. I'd known for several years that they weren't happy together. Those constant rows drove me out of the house so that, in the end, I spent as little time as possible at home. I did my homework and revision in the reference library but it didn't help that they closed at six two evenings a week."

It was, therefore, not surprising that Richard's A-level results were disappointing. "The only one I got was maths – that was the one that didn't need nearly so much revision. So, I didn't get the two D grades I needed to get onto the business studies degree course at the polytechnic. I think what upset me most about my results was the complete incomprehension on the part of my parents – they didn't even realise that they were, in part, to blame."

For a time Richard felt bitter. "It wasn't until I sat down and really talked my situation through with the careers officer that I saw a way through. My ultimate goal is to manage a large store for one of the big chains. I'd first become interested in retailing through a Saturday job in the High Street. Then I saw an article about just how quickly graduates can get on with some of the major stores and decided that it was for me."

The careers officer explained to Richard how good the opportunities were for A-level recruits too and she encouraged him to write to the personnel department at a couple of local department stores. "One of them interviewed me almost immediately and I was offered a place on their A-level management training scheme."

"And now I'm at the polytechnic, although I'm not doing the course I originally intended. I'm on day release doing a BTEC Higher National course in business studies. At work, I'm on a series of three month placements in different parts of the store to learn what each part of the business does. Currently I'm working in the electrical goods department and the next placement will be in the general office. I reckon I'm going to get there anyway – just by a different route. And when it comes to promotion later on, I'll have had three years extra experience over those who've come in on the graduate training scheme!"

The training schemes

What can you expect if you are accepted on to a training scheme? While the actual work that you do during training will vary from company to company, there are likely to be features that are common to any formal scheme. You could expect a comprehensive programme lasting for perhaps one to two years during which time you would gain practical experience working in a number of departments, combined with in-service training and possibly a day a week spent in college. The company's training department would be responsible for supervising your programme and your performance would be monitored with regular assessments.

You may wonder just how marketable the skills you will acquire in a company training scheme are.

While certain aspects of any training scheme will be attuned to the specific requirements of the company, there are skills which will be common to any organisation. Generally speaking the expertise you acquire in your organisation should be transferable to a similar type of establishment – the training received in one hotel group should fit you for similar employment in other hotels; banking experience will equip you to transfer to another bank and may well be relevant to a building society or insurance company. Some skills are very marketable and appropriate to many organisations – a training in accountancy for instance could offer job opportunities in banks, hospitals, hotels, retailing, tourism and many other organisations. Some qualifications acquired during training will open doors into a wide variety of organisations – membership of the Institute of Personnel Management (IPM) would be as valid to the recruitment manager of a record company as to the man or woman in charge of the personnel function in a large pharmaceutical concern.

What then should you be looking for if you decide to enter the employment market?

A well-organised training scheme, the opportunity to acquire a professional qualification, and clearly defined career prospects after training are the ideal requirements. While large companies are likely to have training departments with specialist training staff, a smaller firm may be unable to offer such benefits and it will therefore be important to establish just what training will be available, what opportunities there are to acquire a qualification, and what the promotion prospects are. If there is a recognised professional qualification attached to a job, you will be at a disadvantage without it when you want to move elsewhere.

Change and uncertainty have been the hallmark of the employment market in recent years. Gone are the days when the school leaver could train for a job and expect to remain in the same occupation throughout a working life. Sound work experience, a marketable qualification and a flexible approach are therefore the best foundations on which to build a successful future in the workplace.

Handling Interviews – Positive Thinking

An interview is a golden opportunity to persuade an admissions tutor or employer that you are the right candidate for their establishment. Once you have considered all possible options and planned your strategy, an interview will be your goal, and a successful interview culminating in the offer of a place in higher education or further education or a job will be the ultimate aim. Before reaching this happy conclusion there will of course be a number of hurdles to overcome – perhaps half the battle will be the need for you to persuade *yourself* that you are a worthwhile candidate.

Your present setback will certainly have done little to boost your morale, but it should not be allowed to blight your future. Underachievement in examinations can cause acute anxiety when faced with the prospect of an interview. There is no point in attempting to sweep your results under the carpet but on the other hand you should not feel that you must spend the foreseeable future apologising for them. An interviewer will doubtless be aware from your application (unless you have been unwise enough to conceal it) that you have not been entirely successful in your examinations. If you are invited for interview it is clear that he or she is still prepared to consider you.

You may feel that your situation is unique. It is not. And it is unlikely to be so in the eyes of admissions tutors or employers who are quite used to students with varying degrees of examination attainment. In fact, who knows, he or she may well have been in a similar situation in the past or have had a son or daughter in the same circumstances. This does not mean that you will not be faced with searching questions about your academic record, as this will undoubtedly be an issue which arises on each occasion. Make it a priority before even reaching the point of an interview to consider how you would cope with a probing investigation into your results and give careful thought as to how you would present your case. Once you have tackled this problem you should feel more confident about making applications.

Your first move is to prepare a brief summary of your assessment of the reasons for your situation and how you propose to overcome it. Make a note of the salient points and mentally rehearse what you would say to an imaginary interviewer. The next step is to build up a positive image of yourself by preparing a personal profile which will not only stand you in good stead when making applications, but should also boost your self-confidence. It is easy to underestimate the significance of aspects of your life other than the academic ones when so much importance has been attached to your studies in recent years. Academic ability is, however, only one fact of life and should not be allowed to overshadow your other abilities. So, don't lose sight of your non-academic achievements and personal qualities, concentrate on them rather than the negative aspects of your life.

You could use the basic formula outlined below as a guide for your personal profile and expand on the examples to suit your own circumstances.

1. Personality ....Are you cheerful, hardworking, trustworthy, attentive to detail, etc.?

2. Skills and aptitudes ....Have you, for example, creative or mechanical abilities?

3. Social skills ....Are you persuasive? Do people confide in you because you are a good listener?

4. Organisational ability ....Are you a well organised person? Are you good at organising others?

5. Specialised knowledge ....Do you have, for example, expertise in a foreign language?

6. Positions of responsibility .....Have you been entrusted with any particular responsibilities, either at school or in any other organisation?

7. Socially useful involvement ...Have you been concerned with helping others, such as young or handicapped people or the elderly, perhaps under the auspices of a school, youth or church group?

8. Interests ....In what activities do you
                                         participate?
                                         Sports, music, etc. What are your
                                         hobbies?

The more you know about yourself, your strengths and your weaknesses, the better prepared you will be to face an interviewer. Do not undervalue yourself. Invite the co-operation of family and friends as you compile your personal profile, so that false modesty does not cause you to omit any attainments or positive aspects. Once you have convinced yourself of your own worth you will be ready to convince others that you are worth interviewing.

It is an achievement in itself to be called for interview. Successful communication with the 'powers that be' – academics or employers – will help you towards that interview. First impressions *do* count and it is vital that they are favourable whether you are making contact by telephone, in person, or by letter. It will be particularly important in your case to compensate for any academic deficiencies by making a good initial impression.

Communication by telephone can be a nerve-racking experience during which time a rapid assessment, which could have a 'make or break' effect, is made of you. Brevity and clarity will impress – incoherent rambling will not. Rehearse beforehand, therefore, what you wish to say and have relevant information (such as an advertisement) and a written checklist of questions in front of you.

The written application

Take trouble over written applications – they can require ingenuity and imagination.

A neatly presented application form or a curriculum vitae (CV for short) and a well written letter highlighting relevant details are essential, particularly if your qualifications are not impressive. The rigmarole of answering the questions on an application form can be daunting, but it pays dividends to read through the entire form carefully before putting pen to paper. A careless application is usually the death knell to a possible interview. Many applicants are rejected merely from their written application, so take extra special care before submitting yours, and check for neatness and accuracy.

Tips on how to prepare a CV or set out a letter of application can be found in publications such as the booklets, *Which Way* or *On the Right Track* which are widely available in schools – both booklets were published by the Manpower Services Commission. Make use of your personal profile when required to supply personal details or information of a non-academic nature. This is your opportunity to promote yourself and use it to your advantage.

Try not to be too despondent about the rejections that you are bound to meet along the way, and on no account give up. Most people, irrespective of qualifications find that they have to make a number of applications before they have success.

Invited for interview

So you've got an interview, and with it the chance to prove yourself. First interviews can cause undue anxiety, particularly when there is the additional worry of explaining unsatisfactory results. But there are techniques which can be acquired to help you, so that you stand out from other candidates.

Preparation is the keynote to any interview. You will feel less daunted if you are well prepared. Find out beforehand as much as you can about the course and college or job and company. Scrutinise prospectuses, job specifications and company literature, and if possible do some extra research. Once again refer to your careers office or library for course details, and the Jobcentre, Citizens' Advice Bureau or local Chamber of Commerce for job and company information. The better informed you are the more confident you will feel. If you have had previous interviews of any kind draw on these experiences and avoid any mistakes that you made then.

There is an element of salesmanship involved in an interview – certainly not high pressure salesmanship which usually antagonises – but rather skilful marketing. You must package yourself particularly effectively to counteract any doubts on the part of the 'consumer' (the interviewer) about the quality of the 'product' (*you*).

A mock interview conducted by a careers adviser, parent, or competent friend would give useful practice in answering the type of questions that you are likely to be asked. The threat of the unexpected always lurks in any interview but you will feel less thrown by the occasional awkward question if you have at least planned how you will reply to those that are most likely to crop up. No two interviews are the same but there are common factors which are usually covered. Base your preparation on replies to such questions as these:

1. Why do you want to study this subject/or do this job?
2. Why do you wish to study at this university, polytechnic, college?
   Why do you wish to work for this firm?
3. What were your reasons for your choice of A-levels/Highers?
4. Can you explain the reasons for your examination results?
5. What did you like best/dislike about school?
6. Are you interested in any particular aspect of the course/the job?
7. What contribution do you think you could make to the college/company?
8. What is your ultimate career ambition?
9. Describe yourself/your family?
10. What do you do in your leisure time?

Your answer to question number four needs particular preparation. Be truthful. Be positive. And stress what you have done to come to terms with the disappointment. Show that you have thought through your new course of action.

Keep abreast of the times by looking out for anything concerning your chosen subject of study or career in newspapers or other media, as you may be asked to discuss current issues.

An interview is not usually a one-sided interrogation and there should be an opportunity for you to ask questions. Think of a few and if you are likely to forget them in the heat of the moment, write them down. Your questions can be as revealing to the interviewer as your answers, so make sure that they are sensible and relevant.

The good impression

The day of the interview dawns and you are ready to put your preparations to the test. Make sure that you have the correct time and place, and check your route. Decide what you will wear in advance and make sure that it is ready. It makes sense to dress appropriately for the occasion, and while a casual appearance may fit the bill for a college place, more formal attire will usually make a better impression for a job interview. Always be neat, clean and tidy, with a pleasant smile and a polite manner. Listen carefully to questions and answer clearly. Steer a course between the garrulous and the monosyllabic "no" or "yes". When the question of your results arises just look directly at the interviewer and give as convincing a reply as possible based on what you have already planned to say. A frank approach will be more endearing than attempts at concealment or a litany of complaints about school or teachers. Remember to be positive about yourself and your assets throughout the interview. Evidence of motivation, commitment and enthusiasm will be looked for by the interviewer.

After the interview is over it is a good idea to take stock of your performance and to make a note of any points that might help to improve your technique on another occasion. It would of course be a pleasant surprise to find that this is unnecessary but if you do not succeed at first consider it as a useful experience from which to learn, and 'try, try, try again'!

Further Counselling

The time has come to make a decision, and yet you seem no nearer to a solution. What is to be done? First and foremost – don't panic!

Important decisions are rarely easy and doubtless your original plan was not reached overnight. It is much better to take your time rather than be panicked into the wrong decision. Somewhere there will be a niche for you, even if it is not immediately obvious. But the answer to your problem is more likely to dawn on you gradually rather than in a blinding flash of realisation. Take heart from the fact that it is quite usual for students at a much later stage in their studies to be still uncertain of their future direction, so aim to make decisions step by step and keep your options open as long as possible. As with a jigsaw, patience and a logical and painstaking approach will be required.

So far you have considered what went wrong and have studied the options now available, but there are vital pieces of the 'jigsaw' still missing. To complete the picture you must not overlook your own interests and aptitudes, your values and your personality, for it is not only ability and achievement which make for success. And there is also the enthusiasm which is sparked off by your own particular personality – it is this element which directs people of similar ability and attainment into quite different occupations.

Take for instance the case of Alison and Andrew, both with A-levels in science subjects. Alison who has an enquiring and analytical mind sets her sights on medical research, while Andrew with his concern for the welfare of others and a strong practical streak opted for osteopathy. Consider also David and Janet with similar academic achievements in arts subjects who joined the same large company as trainees at the same time. David who has an outgoing and persuasive personality favoured the retail management aspect of the company while Janet with her flair for dealing with people and her good organising abilities was channeled into personnel management.

Careers counselling

Self-awareness is a crucial factor in any career decision and a greater understanding of yourself will help you to avoid the pitfall of choosing a quite unsuitable occupation. How then do you develop this quality? For many people it is only achieved by a combination of time and experience. It is, however, possible to speed up the process, and a consultation with an experienced careers counsellor could help to give you that sense of direction which at present you feel you lack.

Careers counselling is more than just a chat. It aims, with the help of objective tests, to highlight your strengths and weaknesses and to offer vocational guidance based on an assessment of your aptitudes, ability and personality. The careers counsellor will systematically analyse these factors and will help you identify appropriate occupational areas. You may already have had experience at school of tests designed to assess your aptitudes as opposed to your academic ability – tests are intended to provide some personal insight and equip you for making career decisions. The tests used by a careers counsellor will probably be more extensive and will probe more deeply into aspects of yourself of which you may not have been aware. They will be used as a basis on which to build a positive and constructive plan for your future. The counsellor will discuss the test results with you during what could be a lengthy interview (or a series of interviews), and will make recommendations about appropriate educational and career areas.

Tests and how they work

It is quite usual to be asked to provide details of your personal history in the form of a questionnaire or essay prior to a consultation. This serves the dual purpose of providing information and encouraging you to start thinking about yourself in a systematic way.

The tests bear no resemblance to school examinations where you pass or fail, and should not be a source of worry. What they should do is to help you reach a greater understanding of yourself, so that you are in a better position to make these crucial decisions.

Interest tests

There are interest tests which usually cover seven major activities.

1. Artistic – this includes not only creative ability, but also aesthetic appreciation.

72

2. Computational – this deals with numeracy.
3. Literary – a measurement of how well you express ideas and feelings through words.
4. Persuasive – your influence on others to accept ideas, services or goods.
5. Practical – this is concerned not only with practical skills but with a practical approach to life.
6. Scientific – a curiosity to investigate how and why things happen.
7. Welfare – a concern to help others.

Aptitude tests

There are aptitude tests which provide an insight into your potential for grasping new ideas and developing new skills, and which include verbal reasoning, numerical reasoning and mechanical reasoning. These will assess how well you understand ideas expressed in words and in numbers, your ability to cope with spatial and mechanical concepts, and how attentive you are to detail and accuracy.

Personality tests

There are personality tests designed to establish how you react to different situations and problems, and which indicate whether you are outgoing or reserved, independent-minded or conformist, sensitive or hard-headed, stable or insecure.

Interpretation and advice

Your tests will be interpreted for you by the counsellor who will discuss their implications and present you with a personal profile. Before making recommendations other factors must also be considered. Your own attitudes, your physical make-up and your personal circumstances will clearly have a bearing on your final decision. Your likely level of achievement will depend not only on ability, interest and aptitude, but also on such factors as motivation and determination.

It sounds quite complicated – as indeed it is – but a skilled and sympathetic counsellor should help you to define the kind of work to which you are best suited and make positive suggestions. You should be offered advice about courses, and the level at which it is realistic to aim, and about the specific career areas you should be considering. The type of organisation to which you would best be suited could also be suggested as the same type of work is available in different organisations – a career in computing for example could offer the opportunity to work in organisations as diverse as banks and insurance companies, hospitals and the police force, the entertainment business or the tourist industry.

Careers counsellors do not, however, offer a placement service, and you yourself will therefore be responsible for putting the theory into practice.

After a consultation a report will usually be provided which will include the results of the various tests and the recommendations. There should also be information about any possibilities that you discussed and how to set about finding out about them.

Why then, you may ask, if such advice is available, is everyone not automatically assessed in this way at school, so that they can be 'pegged' into the right holes and avoid wasting valuable time floundering around in a state of indecision? One reason is that however objective and scientific the tests, human personality is so complex that they cannot offer a definitive solution. If they did everyone would be flocking to the careers counsellors. So many factors have to be taken into consideration, and the tests are only one part of the process. Some find tests and counselling provide the answer to their dilemma. For others it is less successful and perhaps merely serves to underline what they already know and sheds little new light on the situation.

The quality of advice too can vary considerably, and your relationship with the counsellor can affect how you will react to recommendations. It may not be sufficient, therefore, to rely completely on careers counselling, but to regard it as a signpost towards your final destination.

Who can help you then if you do decide that careers counselling is right for you? Your local careers service may provide a free counselling service which includes the use of tests. Some services make use of the CASCAID test which links interests to careers. For more in-depth testing it may be necessary to approach a privately run vocational guidance service and pay a consultation fee.

Before embarking on careers counselling it is important to

check the credentials of the organisation and its counsellors. Make enquiries about the use of tests, the length of discussion time at your disposal, the availability of up-to-date careers literature and the provision of a report. The tests offered can vary in depth and intensity as does the time devoted to a personal interview. It can also be an expensive and time-consuming process. The skill and experience of the counsellor who interprets the tests is of paramount importance and therefore a reliable recommendation from someone with personal experience of a counsellor would be useful. It may be that your school can advise you in this matter.

Self-help

Even if it is not possible to have a session with a careers counsellor you can still develop your own self-awareness by considering some of the points mentioned in connection with the tests. Analyse the personal qualities required for various jobs as outlined in an up-to-date careers book and try to link them to your own. This might at least help you to eliminate the areas that are likely to be unsuitable and concentrate on a nucleus of possibility. Other available 'tools' are the computerised information systems which may be available in your school or college, in the local library or the careers service. Access to JIIG/CAL (Job Ideals and Information Generator/ Computer Assisted Learning) would help to identify broad areas of work in which you might be interested, and provide ideas and information about suggested jobs.

There is, alas, no crystal ball to guide you on your way! If, however, you have done your best to develop your self-awareness and to match yourself as a person to the most suitable educational or occupational areas, then the time is probably ripe to 'take the plunge' and make a decision.

Sources of help

The British Psychological Society,
St Andrews House,
48 Princess Road East,
Leicester LE1 7DR   0533 549568

The above organisation can supply a list of names and addresses of its members who provide vocational guidance services. It is merely a list and should not be taken to be a recommendation.

Vocational Guidance Consultants

Career and Educational Counselling,
The Tavistock Centre,
120 Belsize Lane,
London NW3 5BA   01-794 1309

Career Analysts Vocational Guidance Service,
Career House,
90 Gloucester Place,
London W1H 4BL   01-935 5452

Career Counselling Services,
46 Ferry Road,
London SW13   01-741 0335

Careers and Educational Guidance,
28 Compton Avenue,
Gidea Park,
Romford,
Essex RM2 6ET   0708 46700

Career Guidance,
5 Arlington Court,
Kenton Avenue,
Gosforth,
Newcastle upon Tyne   091 284 1814

Career Guidance Consultants,
Hooton Lawn,
Benty Heath Lane,
Hooton,
Merseyside   051 327 3894

Career Guidance Ltd,
Bloomsbury Square,
London WC1   01-242 3551

Career Plan Ltd.,
Chichester House,
Chichester Rents,
Chancery Lane,
London WC2A 1EG   01-242 5775

Gabbitas Truman & Thring Counselling Service,
Broughton House,
6–8 Sackville Street,
Piccadilly,
London W1X 2BR   01-734 0161/01-439 2071

Independent Assessment and Research Centre,
57 Marylebone High Street,
London W1M 3AE   01-486 6106

Independent Schools Careers Organisation,
12a–18a Princess Way,
Camberley,
Surrey GU15 3SP   0276 21188

National Advisory Centre on Careers for Women,
Drayton House,
30 Gordon Street,
London WC1J 0AX   01-380 0117

Percy Coutts & Co.,
25 Whitehall,
London SW1A 2BS   01-839 2271

Vocational Guidance Association,
7 Harley House,
Upper Harley Street,
London NW1 4RP   01-935 2600

Vocational Guidance Centre,
4 St Ann's Square,
Manchester M2 7HF   061 832 7671

Taking time off

There are undoubtedly attractions about taking time off from study, especially when faced by the need to rethink your future. Decisions taken in haste can lead to mistakes when your judgment is clouded by a sense of urgency. A break from educational routine can put your life into perspective and for some people it will be an enriching experience. It is not always the right choice, however, and it is sensible to weigh up the pros and cons before making a decision.

Possible advantages

Time to think

As you are in the position of having to take a fresh look at your plans for the future, a break now could give you breathing space to decide the appropriate direction for you.

Maturity

Most students who take time off at this stage in their lives find it a valuable experience. The opportunity to do something quite different and to escape from the confines of the academic environment broadens horizons. To meet, for the first time possibly, and work with people from a background other than your own develops and matures the personality.

Independence

For those who have never been away from home for any length of time a period of travel, for instance, could give you a chance to stand on your own feet and to cope with running your own life. To earn money in what may be your first job offers a sense of independence.

Practical value

If you are likely to improve your results by retaking some subjects it will be to your advantage to take time off to prepare. Profitable use of your time to gain experience in the area where you think you would like to make your future will usually impress a prospective employer or admissions tutor. A job related to your chosen career will give you an insight into whether it really is the right field for you. Employment in a business or industrial environment with a view to a course in business studies would be the type of experience which would be considered relevant. Work or study abroad could help you improve or learn a new language, while voluntary work for a charitable organisation should provide a valuable foundation for a future in a 'caring' profession.

Once in a lifetime

Once qualified and in permanent employment it becomes much more difficult to take time out, and you may never again be in the situation where such a lengthy break is feasible. A pipedream to explore Australia could be realised – an opportunity to get the wanderlust out of your system!

Motivation

Decisions about your future made with a background of greater experience and with a new self-confidence and maturity are more likely to motivate you to succeed in your chosen course, whether it is in higher education or employment. It can be fun and very refreshing to try out a number of different activities. Constructive time out is usually a beneficial experience and if you have shown enterprise, should find favour in the eyes of a future employer or admissions tutor.

Disadvantages

Disorganised drifting

There is a danger that the time out can be frittered away doing very little. You are unlikely to benefit from 'dropping out' and for some students it may result in a loss of motivation and an inability to pick up the threads of study again. It will also not look impressive in any future application.

Loss of working routine

It can be difficult to settle back into the pattern of study, and for some it might be better to consider time off between leaving higher education and taking up employment. Certain subjects too, such as mathematics, seem to benefit from unbroken study.

Duration of course

If you have plans to embark on a lengthy course of study such as architecture or medicine you may not wish for any delay in gaining your qualifications.

Attitudes of higher education institutions

Some admissions tutors consider constructive time out as a valuable experience, while others are not in favour of a break from study. You should certainly check their attitude before making plans to delay further study, if there is any likelihood of acceptance onto a course in spite of your results.

Ideas for using the time in the U.K.

Paid work

The availability of paid temporary employment varies in different areas of the country. In some there will be opportunities if you are prepared to take time and trouble to look for them, while in others it will be more difficult. The 'Situations Vacant' column of your local newspaper is one possible source, as is the local Jobcentre or careers office. The latter will also be able to give details of the government's Youth Training Scheme, should you still be young enough to be eligible. Private employment agencies, usually to be found in most sizeable towns, can be useful sources of temporary work – some specialise in office jobs, some in manual work. The acquisition of typing skills is a bonus when applying for office jobs, but clerical vacancies exist too. Shops usually take on extra staff over the pre-Christmas and sales periods. Exhibition centres and festivals can also be fruitful areas for the job-seeker.

In regions of high unemployment or remote parts of the country where it may be difficult to find a job, it might be worth applying

for seasonal work in another part of the country, so long as
accommodation is provided – for example, hotel work, fruit picking
on a farm, or work in a holiday camp.

You may not have realised you can gain experience in the
Armed Forces for a short period. The Army and Royal Marines,
through School Service Liaison Officers offer Short Service Limited
Commissions (for young men prior to going on to further education) –
five months minimum service for Army and nine months for the
Royal Marines.

If you are looking for temporary work it often pays to let as
many people as possible know that you are in the job market, as
opportunities can arise through friends, relatives, or chance contacts.

Voluntary work

Volunteer work offers an interesting and challenging alternative –
opportunities existing both in the long and the short-term. A wide
variety of projects of a community and environmental nature
welcome school leavers. Free board and lodging is usually available
for volunteers required to live away from home, although some
projects do require a small contribution, and pocket money and
expenses are normally provided.

The period of commitment will vary, most organisations
requiring at least a few months availability. Although it has the
disadvantage of being unpaid, a period spent in voluntary service
can be a very rewarding experience from the personal point of
view. It brings a fresh outlook to your life and puts your own
problems into perspective. It will certainly be more stimulating
than time spent in the routine of a dull and monotonous job.

A number of organisations welcome volunteers for a variety of
social work with for instance children, disabled people, or the
homeless. A starting point for this type of work would be Community
Service Volunteers, 237 Pentonville Road, London N1 9NJ
(Tel. 01-278 6601); CSV co-ordinate voluntary service for young
people nationwide. Short-term workcamps are run by the National
Trust, and the Church of England (Cathedral Camps). Your own
local area may have a Council for Voluntary Service which would
be worth contacting – information should be available at the Citizens'
Advice Bureau.

Courses

Time between can be used to acquire practical skills. The ability to type, to cook and to drive will stand you in good stead, whether you are male or female. Most local authority colleges of further education offer typing and cookery courses, and short intensive courses are usually available in private colleges in large towns. The latter can, however, be expensive. Driving schools are to be found in most areas. A qualification in teaching English as a foreign language (TEFL) can be useful if you have plans to work abroad later, or wish to earn money teaching foreign students in this country.

Ideas for activities abroad

Paid work

Many enterprising young people find ways of working their passage around the world. With some earnings from a job at home in your pocket you may have sufficient to set off for foreign parts and pick up odd jobs to keep body and soul together as you travel. Often this work will be casual as work permits (which may be difficult to obtain) are frequently required in non-EEC countries. For linguists, the Central Bureau for Educational Visits and Exchanges, Seymour Mews House, Seymour Mews, London W14 9E (Tel. 01-486 5101) may offer opportunities. Working as an au pair in a family is a good way of learning or improving a foreign language and advertisements for this type of work appear in *The Lady* magazine.

Leaflets giving advice on employment prospects and listing agencies which offer work are available in some national tourist offices in this country. The best contacts though can be friends or relatives living abroad.

Some of the following organisations could be approached for the type of work and the countries in which they specialise.

1. Camp America – 37a Queens Gate, London SW7 5HR (Tel. 01-589-3223), recruits students to help in childrens' holiday camps in the U.S.A. Air transport, board and pocket money are provided.
2. Canvas Holidays, Bull Plain, Hertford SG14 1DY

(Tel. 0992 553535) employs residential couriers on campsites in Europe.

3. Jobs in the Alps, P.O. Box 388, London SW1X 8LX provides seasonal work in winter or summer in Alpine resorts.

4. Projects 67, 36 Great Russell Street, London WC1B 3PP (Tel. 01-636 1262), offers Kibbutz opportunities and archaeological digs in Israel.

Voluntary work abroad

Opportunities for school leavers to do voluntary work overseas are now extremely limited, graduates and newly qualified professional people being required in developing countries. International Voluntary Service, 53 Regent Road, Leicester LE1 6YL, (Tel. 0533 541862), would be a contact for this type of work. Some church-based organisations also offer voluntary work abroad.

Courses

Linguistic and cultural courses for foreigners exist in many countries. They are often costly. Embassies and government tourist offices in this country can usually provide such information. The Central Bureau for Educational Visits and Exchanges (addresses given earlier) publishes a useful booklet.

Why time off?

Do give careful consideration as to whether this is the right time for you to have a break from study, or whether it would make more sense to delay it until after completion of a course. Don't view it as a soft option or an easy way to postpone hard decisions. If it does seem to be right for you, decide how you will spend these months, and plan accordingly. Avoid treating it as a prolonged holiday. It should be a time of growth – growth in self-confidence and self-sufficiency. It will be a bonus, if you can make discoveries not only about far-flung places, but about yourself.

Taking a year off

You will find a lively comprehensive look at time out in *Taking a Year Off* by Val Butcher and Chris Swanson, and published by Trotman and Company Limited.

Other Useful Publications

A Year Off . . . A Year On – CRAC, Hobsons Publishing PLC, Bateman Street, Cambridge CB2 1LZ; *Jobs in the GAP Year* – ISCO, 12a–18a Princess Way, Camberley, Surrey GU15 3SP; *Summer Jobs Britain*, *Summer Jobs Abroad*, and *Work Your Way around the World*, published by Vacation Work, Oxford (available from booksellers). The Central Bureau for Educational Visits and Exchanges (address already given) also has a number of relevant publications.

Booklist

Career choice

After School: A Guide to Post School Opportunities, Felicity Taylor.
Kogan Page, 120 Pentonville Road, London N1 9JN.
Careers Encyclopaedia, edited by Audrey Segal. Cassel PLC, Artillery
House, Artillery Row, London SW1P 1RT.
Decisions at 17/18, CRAC, Hobsons Press, Bateman Street,
Cambridge CB2 1LZ.
Equal Opportunities – A Careers Guide, Ruth Miller and Anna Alston.
Penguin Books Ltd., Harmondsworth, Middlesex.
Focus at 18, Newpoint Publishing Co. Ltd., Newpoint House, St
James' Lane, London N10 3DF.
How to Choose a Career, Vivien Donald. Kogan Page, 120
Pentonville Road, London N1 9JN.
The Job Book, Hobsons Press, Bateman Street, Cambridge
CB2 1LZ.
Jobs and Careers after A-levels, Mary Munro. CRAC, Hobsons Press,
Bateman Street, Cambridge CB2 1LZ.
Opportunities '89, Careers and Occupational Information Centre,
Moorfoot, Sheffield S1 4PQ.
Routes into the Media, Trotman and Company Ltd., 12–14 Hill
Rise, Richmond, Surrey TW10 6UA.
Routes into Retail and Distribution, Trotman and Company Ltd. (see
above).
Routes into the Built Environment, Trotman and Company Ltd. (see
above).
Routes into the Health Service, Trotman and Company Ltd. (see
above).

Higher education

*A Compendium of Advanced Courses in Colleges of Further and Higher
Education; Full-time and Sandwich Courses in Polytechnics and
Colleges Outside the University Sector*, London and Home Counties
Regional Advisory Council for Further Education, Tavistock House
South, Tavistock Square, London WC1H 9LR.

Directory of Further Education, CRAC, Hobsons Press, Bateman Street, Cambridge CB2 1LZ.

Directory of First Degree and Diploma of Higher Education Courses, available free from the Council for National Academic Awards (CNAA), 344–354 Gray's Inn Road, London WC1X 8BP.

Guide to the Colleges and Institutes of Higher Education 1988, Administrative Officer, Standing Conference of Principals, Edge Hill College of Higher Education, St Helen's Road, Ormskirk, Lancashire L39 4QP.

Getting into Colleges and Institutes of Higher Education, Trotman and Company Ltd., 12–14 Hill Rise, Richmond, Surrey TW10 6UA.

Getting into Polytechnics, Trotman and Company (see above).

Getting into University, Brian Heap and Stephen Lamley. Trotman and Company Ltd. (see above).

Polytechnic Courses Handbook, available from the Committee of Directors of Polytechnics, Kirkman House, 12–14 Whitfield Street, London W1P 6AX. A list of all polytechnic courses with details of subjects studied throughout each course. Published annually.

UCCA, PO Box 28, Cheltenham, Glos GL50 1HY. This handbook is free and usually distributed through schools, colleges, etc. to applicants. Published annually.

PCAS Guide for Applicants. Available from the Polytechnics Central Admissions System, PO Box 67, Cheltenham, Glos GL50 3AP. This handbook is free and is usually available through schools and colleges. Published annually.

CRCH booklet. Information booklet giving details of all degree and other advanced courses within the Central Register and Clearing House scheme (includes all public-sector undergraduate initial teacher training courses in England and Wales). Available from schools and colleges for those in full-time education: otherwise free of charge from the Central Register and Clearing House, 3 Crawford Place, London W1H 2BN.

Design Courses in Britain, Design Council, 28 Haymarket, London SW1Y 2SU.

Scottish Central Institutions Handbook, Paisley College of Technology, High Street, Paisley PA1 2BE, Scotland.

DON'T PANIC
– About Disappointing A-level Results/Highers

Fiona Smith

That innocuous looking little brown envelope containing A-level, AS-level or Highers results may be dreaded by many students. For some it is the bearer of good news: the right grades have been obtained to be able to take up a conditional offer of a place on a course. For others it brings disappointment and bewilderment. And it is for *these* students that Fiona Smith draws upon her wealth of experience in careers guidance to offer sound advice and, most importantly, encouragement.

Don't Panic examines the options including:
- retakes
- a change of career plan
- alternative courses
- employment
- the possibility of still taking the original course

The author addresses the problem of where students can turn for help and how they may be able to come to terms with what they may see as 'failure'. And throughout the keynote is in the title, *Don't Panic…*

TROTMAN

Published by
Trotman and Company Limited
12 – 14 Hill Rise
Richmond
Surrey
TW10 6UA

ISBN 0-85660-140-3

£4.95

9 780856 601408

Where to Eat

CORNWALL

The Pandora Inn, Restronguet Creek, Mylor Bridge, Falmouth

first edition
eating places for all occasions and budgets